TWAYNE'S WORLD AUTHORS SERIES
A Survey of the World's Literature

PUERTO RICO

Luis Davila, Indiana University
EDITOR

René Marqués

TWAS 516

RENÉ MARQUÉS

By ELEANOR J. MARTIN

Rutgers—The State University

TWAYNE PUBLISHERS

A DIVISION OF G. K. HALL & CO. BOSTON

Published in 1979 by Twayne Publishers,
A division of G. K. Hall & Co.
All Rights Reserved

Printed on permanent/durable acid-free paper and bound
in the United States of America

First Printing

Library of Congress Cataloging in Publication Data

Martin, Eleanor J
René Marqués.

(Twayne's world authors series ; TWAS 516 :
Puerto Rico)
Bibliography: p. 159–64
Includes index.
1. Marqués, René—Criticism and interpretation.
PQ7439.M265Z77   868   78–15518
ISBN 0–8057–6357–0

Contents

About the Author

After studying at Hunter College of CUNY, Eleanor J. Martin received her doctorate in Puerto Rican literature from New York University. Since receipt of her Ph.D., she has been teaching at Rutgers University, where she specializes in courses in Latin American literature and in the Spanish literature of the Golden Age. She is widely-published, having contributed articles in both fields to several leading journals: *Revista Chicano-Riqueña, Latin American Theater Review, Journal of Popular Culture, Revista-Review* of the Interamerican University of Puerto Rico, *Bulletin of the Comediantes, Modern Language Notes, Papeles de Son Armadans, Forum for Modern Language Study, Kentucky Romance Quarterly.* Since 1977, she has moderated the section on Puerto Rican literature at conventions (annual) of the American Popular Culture Association, where she has promoted the work of not only Islanders, but also that of the "New Yoricans" of her native city.

Preface

The artistic production of Puerto Rican writer René Marqués to date includes fifteen dramas, three collections of short stories, two novels, two volumes of essays, and a book of poetry.[1] All of his work is, in one way or another, a social commentary on Puerto Rican society and on the larger human community.

In his work, Marqués laments Puerto Rico's colonial status, a historical fact for over four centuries. First a colony of Spain, Puerto Rico was ceded to the United States as a result of the War of 1898. U.S. citizenship was granted to the islanders by the Jones Act of 1917. However, the first local government, based on a popular election of their chief executive, was not instituted until 1947. In 1952, under Governor Luis Muñoz Marín, Puerto Rico became a commonwealth (Estado Libre Asociado) of the United States, a status it retains today. As a commonwealth, Puerto Rico enjoys neither statehood nor independence. Although citizens of the United States, the islanders neither vote in presidential elections nor pay federal taxes. Puerto Rican men are, however, subject to obligatory military service in the U.S. armed forces. In the United States Congress, Puerto Rico is represented by a resident commissioner, who has a voice but no vote. The United States maintains control over many vital aspects of Puerto Rican life, including defense, customs, migration, mail, merchant marine, minimum wages,[2] and so forth.

An ardent defender of Puerto Rico's liberty from the United States, Marqués dramatizes the perils of colonial status and calls for political resistance. He delves into the islanders' rationale — past and present — for offering minimal resistance to foreign domination and analyzes society's suppression of liberation efforts.

Marqués views submission to United States domination as a forfeiture of political sovereignty for economic gain. Since the advent of the 1940s, Puerto Rico has been increasingly industrialized by the United States. U.S. dollars pouring into Puerto Rico have transformed the island from a once impoverished agrarian community into a complex industrial entity. Contented with the material benefits provided by northern industrialization of the island, many Puerto Ricans are reluctant to sever political ties with the United States. Marqués deplores the choice of what historian Gordon K. Lewis has termed "a political status that provides food with shame" over "one that offers poverty with dignity"[3] and attributes this choice to man's instinctual satisfaction of his material needs at the expense of the spiritual. Marqués dramatizes this tendency in the context of past and present, in biblical times as well as in modern society.

Marqués is no mere propagandist. As a writer he is closely linked with twentieth century trends in drama and fiction. His literature studies in Spain (1946) and at New York's Piscator's Dramatic Workshop (1949) familiarized him with contemporary literary forms and their practitioners in Europe and the Americas. In his drama, Marqués has experimented with a variety of theatrical styles: naturalistic drama, ballet or pantomime, allegory, poetic theater, theater of the absurd, and expressionistic and existentialist drama. His work reflects the influence of such writers as Ortega y Gasset, Unamuno, Faulkner, Pirandello, Sartre, O'Neill, Beckett, Ionesco, and Camus.

Marqués scoffs at "influence study," telling critics that they are free to attribute to him whatever influences they choose.[4] Mindful of this, I will not in this study hazard conjectures as to specific influences on the author. I will rather demonstrate how Marqués adapts the inventory of techniques, traditions, and genres that are available to him as a modern writer to suit his own political and humanistic purposes.

I have grouped Marqués' writing between the years 1946 and 1970 into nondramatic (Chapters 2-5) and dramatic (Chapters 6-9) work. A brief account of Marqués' life and times should be read along with Chapters 2-4, for Marqués' first novel, poetry, and essays are inextricably linked with Puerto Rican social issues and reflect the development of the social views that are so central to Marqués' drama. I have considered Marqués' stylistic development in these genres, as well as in the short story (Chapter 5). Marqués' drama draws on much of the thematic and stylistic qualities of his nondramatic works. After discussing Marqués' two early experimental plays (Chapter 6), I have analyzed Marqués' more mature drama, which is grouped by themes: social, social-existential, biblical (Chapters 7-9). While I was making final revisions on the manuscript, Marqués published a second novel and a third collection of short stories. Since the time span between the first and second novel is nineteen years, and between the second and third collection of short stories, fourteen years, indicating a change in ideology and in some cases, style, I thought it best to discuss these works in a final chapter (10).

I am deeply grateful to René Marqués for permission to quote from his work. I only regret his "silence" in answer to requests for more detailed information on his life (especially that of the 1970's). I have analyzed Marqués' published work, omitting one unpublished drama *Palm Sunday* (1949). Translations from his work are mine, with the exception of Dr. Charles Pilditch's translation of Marqués' drama *La carreta (The Oxcart)*. I also wish to thank Professors H. Piñera and H. Rivera of New York University, and Professors F. Dauster and C. Pilditch of Rutgers University for their generous advice, and to credit the tireless editorial efforts of Rima Shore.

Chronology

1919   October 4: Marqués born in Arecibo, grandson of farmers.

1942   Receives degree in agronomy from the Colegio de Agricultura y Artes Mecánicas (College of Agriculture and Mechanical Arts) in Mayagüez. Marries Serena Valesco, whom he divorces fifteen years later.

1944   Publishes *Peregrinación,* a volume of poetry.

1946   Travels to Spain to study literature at the University of Madrid. Writes the drama *El hombre y sus sueños.*

1947   Writes *El sol y los Mac Donald* (drama). Returns to Puerto Rico, and founds and presides over Pro Arte de Arecibo. His reviews appear in *El Mundo;* the journal *Asomante* publishes his literary criticism.

1948   Writes for the *Diario de Puerto Rico. El hombre y sus sueños* appears in *Asomante.*

1949   Accepts a Rockefeller Foundation scholarship to study drama in New York at Columbia University and the Piscator's Dramatic Workshop. Writes the play *Palm Sunday.*

1950   Returns to San Juan, where he writes for the Division of Community Education of the Department of Public Education. *El sol y los Mac Donald* is staged for the first time at the University of Puerto Rico.

1951   Writes *La carreta* (drama). Founds the Experimental Theater of the Ateneo; holds the position of secretary of the board of directors of the Puerto Rican Ateneo.

1953   Becomes director of the editorial unit of the Division of Community Education. *La carreta* is presented in New York and San Juan.

1954   *La carreta* is presented in Caguas, Puerto Rico, in January.

1955   Writes *Juan Bobo y la Dama de Occidente* (drama). Publishes *Otro día nuestro* (short stories).

1956   Writes *La muerte no entrará en palacio* (drama). *Palm Sunday* premieres at the Municipal Theater Tapia of San Juan, directed by Marqués himself. *Juan Bobo y la Dama de Occidente* is published by Editorial Los Presentes of Mexico.

1957   Accepts a Guggenheim scholarship (awarded in 1954) and travels to New York to write his first novel, *La víspera del hombre*. Visits Madrid to attend the premiere of *La carreta* by the National Theater María Guerrero. Visits Palma de Mallorca to meet his father's family. *El sol y los Mac Donald* is published in *Asomante*.

1958　Travels to Mexico City as a member of an official Puerto Rican delegation to the first Interamerican Biennial of Painting. Receives four Ateneo prizes for short story, theater, novel, and essay. Writes *Los soles truncos* (drama), which is presented in San Juan in the First Theater Festival sponsored by the Institute of Puerto Rican Culture, directed by Victoria Espinosa de Maisonet. Also writes *Un niño azul para esa sombra* (drama).

1959　Founds with Eliezer Curet Cuevas the Book Club of Puerto Rico. *Los soles truncos* is produced at the Festival of the Americas in Chicago. Edits *Cuentos puertor/riqueños de hoy* (short stories).

1960　Publishes *En una ciudad llamada San Juan* (short stories). Writes *Carnaval afuera, carnaval adentro* (drama: actual date is uncertain; see Chapter 1, note 3), and *La casa sin reloj* (drama). *Los soles truncos* is produced in Madrid. *Un niño azul para esa sombra* is presented at the Third Theater Festival in San Juan.

1961　*La carreta* is presented at the Fourth Theater Festival in San Juan. Premiere of *La casa sin reloj* in the Experimental Theater of the Ateneo.

1962　*Los soles truncos* is presented in Mexico City. *Carnaval afuera, carnaval adentro* premieres in Havana at the Festival of Latin American Theater.

1964　*Los soles truncos* is presented in San Juan and at the new Calatrava Theater in Salamanca, Spain. Writes *El apartamiento* (drama), which premieres at the Puerto Rican Theater Festival.

1965　Writes *Mariana o el alba* (drama), which premieres in San Juan during the Eighth Puerto Rican Theater Festival.

1966　Publishes *El apartamiento* and *Ensayos* (1953–1966).

1968　Publishes *Mariana o el alba*.

1969　Writes and publishes *Sacrificio en el Monte Moriah* (drama).

1970　*Sacrificio en el Monte Moriah* premieres at the Puerto Rican Theater Festival. Writes and publishes *David y Jonatán —*

Tito y Berenice (Dos dramas de amor, poder, y desamor).

1971   Publishes *Ensayos* (1953–1971), *Carnaval afuera, carnaval adentro*, and *Vía crucis del hombre puertorriqueño* (Oratorio).

1976   *Los soles truncos* is presented in New York at the Grammercy Arts Theater and also at the Penn State Symposium (Oct. 28–30). Publishes his second novel, *La mirada,* and a third collection of short stories, *Inmersos en el silencio.*

1977   Presentation of *Los soles truncos* at the Theater Tapia of San Juan, March 17–April 3.

1978   Presentation of *Los soles truncos* by the Spanish Theatre Repertory Co. in the Gramercy Arts Theatre.

CHAPTER 1

René Marqués: The Man and His Times

R ENÉ Marqués is today one of Puerto Rico's foremost men of
letters. Working in several literary genres, he has won numer-
ous prizes in the Puerto Rican Ateneo, in the United States, and
abroad; and his plays have been produced throughout the world.

I *Life*

Marqués was born in Arecibo on October 4, 1919. His early years
were spent in the home of his maternal grandparents, who instilled
in him their spiritual and ethical values. Two relatives, Dr. Francisco María Susoni and Doña Padrina Padilla de Sanz, fostered in
the adolescent Marqués two supreme values: love for his land and
also for its liberty. Doña Padrina, often known as the Daughter of
the Caribbean (*Hija del Caribe*), was the daughter of the Puerto
Rican poet José Guadalberto Padilla. She too was a poet, as well as
a short story writer and piano teacher, and her Arecibo home was
frequented by writers, musicians, and artists. An ardent defender
of Puerto Rican independence and of woman's rights, she wrote
many articles on political and feminist issues. Doña Padrina
encouraged young Marqués' literary aspirations.

But Marqués was first to become an agriculturalist. The grandson of agronomists, Marqués followed in the family tradition by
earning an agronomy degree from the College of Agriculture and
Mechanical Arts in Mayagüez in 1942. He pursued this career for
two years, working for the Department of Agriculture. A nascent
literary vocation, however, compelled him to travel to Spain in
1946, where he took literature courses at the University of Madrid.
When his "Chronicles from Spain" ("Crónicas de España")
appeared in the Puerto Rican publication *El mundo,* Marqués' literary career was launched. His year in Spain also produced his first

15

two dramas *El hombre y sus sueños* (*Man and His Dreams,* 1946) and *El sol y los Mac Donald* (*The Sun and the MacDonalds,* 1947).[1]

Returning to Puerto Rico, Marqués worked as a manager for Velasco Alonso, Inc. (in the 1940s, Marqués had married Serena Velasco, to whom he was wed for fifteen years). But he did not put aside his literary vocation; he founded and presided over Pro Arte de Arecibo, and his reviews appeared in *El mundo.* The journal *Asomante* published his literary criticism, and by 1948 Marqués was writing for the *Diario de Puerto Rico.* In the same year, *Asomante* published his play *Man and His Dreams.*

Awarded a grant by the Rockefeller Foundation in 1949, Marqués left the *Diario* and came to New York, where he studied drama at Columbia University and at the Piscator's Dramatic Workshop. He wrote in English the play *Palm Sunday* for a course on playwriting given by Dr. Theodore Apstein at Columbia University.

After returning to Puerto Rico, Marqués plunged into a period of intense literary involvement. In 1950, he began to write for the Division of Community Education of the Department of Education, in 1953 becoming the head of its editorial unit — a position that allowed Marqués to sharpen his skills as a filmmaker. In 1951, he founded the Experimental Theater of the Ateneo, which he directed until 1954; at the same time, he served as secretary of the board of directors of the Puerto Rican Ateneo. In 1959, he founded with Eliezer Curet Cuevas the Book Club of Puerto Rico. During this period, Marqués' output of dramas, short stories, and novel was prolific: *Juan Bobo y la Dama de Occidente* (*Juan Bobo and the Lady of the Occident,* 1955); *Otro día nuestro* (*Another Day of Ours,* 1955); *La muerte no entrará en palacio* (*Death Shall Not Enter the Palace,* 1956); *La víspera del hombre* (*The Eve of Manhood,* 1957); *Los soles truncos* (*The Truncated Suns,* 1958); *Un niño azul para esa sombra* (*A Blue Child for that Shadow,* 1958); *Cuentos puertorriqueños de hoy* (*Modern Puerto Rican Short Stories,* 1959). His plays were staged in Puerto Rico, New York, Chicago, and Madrid. In 1957, Marqués' drama *La carreta* (*The Oxcart,* 1951) became the first contemporary Puerto Rican play to be performed in Europe. Marqués traveled extensively: to Madrid in 1957 to attend the première of *The Oxcart* in the National Theater María Guerrero; to Palma de Mallorca to meet his father's family. In the same year he returned to New York where, supported by a Guggenheim fellowship, he wrote the major part of his novel *The Eve of Manhood*. In 1958, he traveled to Mexico City as a member of an official Puerto Rican delegation to the first Interamerican Biennial of Painting.

Marqués' work continued to receive recognition: in 1958 he was awarded Ateneo prizes for achievement in the genres of short story ("La sala" ["The Living Room"]), drama (*A Blue Child for that Shadow*), novel, and essay ("Pesimismo literario y optimismo político: su coexistencia en el Puerto Rico actual" ["Literary Pessimism and Political Optimism in Present-day Puerto Rico"]) — becoming the only Puerto Rican author to win simultaneously four first prizes. His drama *La casa sin reloj (The House Without a Clock)* received first prize in the playwriting competition sponsored by the Puerto Rican Ateneo in 1960; in 1961 *A Blue Child for that Shadow* won the Institute of Puerto Rico's prize for literature; and in 1962 *The Eve of Manhood* received the Iberian-American prize for the novel from the United States William Faulkner Foundation.

II   *Times*

Marqués' work is a mirror of his times; it is particularly a reflection of United States intervention in Puerto Rico's economy, culture, and politics since the turn of the century. Marqués traces in his writings the establishment of a sugar monoculture on the island, which later gave way to "Operation Bootstrap" — the industrialization of Puerto Rico by the U.S. Puerto Rican culture was also dominated by the United States, salient examples being the Americanization of the school system, together with the emphasis placed upon the use of English over the mother tongue. Marqués also records resistance to this intervention, when in the 1930s, a nationalist group, under the leadership of Pedro Albizu Campos, campaigned for Puerto Rico independence. Nationalist uprisings during this epoch, however, were quelled, and Albizu Campos was imprisoned. When nationalist agitation resumed in the 1950s — outbreaks against President Truman in Washington (October 30, 1950) and against Governor Luis Muñoz Marín in the same year — opponents of independence hastened the establishment of the commonwealth (1952) to solidify ties with the United States. The commonwealth has been the order of the day since that time, and governors of Puerto Rico have continually supported strong ties with the United States, either in the form of commonwealth or statehood. (Governors Luis Muñoz Marín [1948–1964] and Rafael Hernández Colón [1972–1976] espoused commonwealth; Governors Luis Ferré [1964–1968] and Carlos Romero Barceló [elected in 1976] support statehood.) Since 1952, then, for Marqués, Puerto Rican dependency on the North has become the official political ideology.

III *Marqués' Reaction to the Times*

Marqués sharply criticizes this attitude on the part of his countrymen. He records the disastrous effects of the establishment of the sugar monoculture in his semiautobiographical novel *The Eve of Manhood*. Marqués also became increasingly alarmed by the economic shift on his island in the 1940s. He considered "Operation Bootstrap" a false and dangerous program for "progress," since it was based on Northern necessities, ignored the agricultural orientation of the island, and by the 1950s, had created wholesale abandonment of the land and widespread migration. Marqués portrayed this wave of migration to the city and to the continent in his drama *The Oxcart* (1951).

In *The Eve of Manhood,* Marqués traced the pattern of Americanization that meant "progress" to some, but to Marqués signaled the loss of Puerto Rican values and the sense of Puerto Rican identity. He decries this increasing contamination of Puerto Rican culture and language in *Ensayos* (*Essays* [1953–1966], later expanded to include essays up to 1971), and he traced the devaluation of indigenous culture in the University of Puerto Rico (a trend begun in the forties, labeled "universalism" and later "occidentalism") in the drama *Juan Bobo and the Lady of the Occident*.

Marqués, of course, sympathizes with the movement for Puerto Rican independence. As an adolescent in the 1930s, he witnessed the emergence of Albizu Campos as leader of the nationalist party. In a prologue to his short story "Otro día nuestro,"[2] Marqués reported that although he neither knew Campos personally nor publicly adhered to his political line, he never openly renounced Campos' policies. In his unpublished play *Palm Sunday,* Marqués dramatized the 1937 Ponce massacre, in which a group of policemen fired on unarmed nationalist demonstrators on Palm Sunday.

Marqués' plays often stage the clash between official and liberation ideology, which invariably ends in the suppression of the independence or revolutionary movement. Yet he does provide "poetic" political alternatives: for example, the fictional assassination of Governor Luis Muñoz Marín (representing the hoped-for death of the commonwealth) and the triumph of the liberation forces in his drama *Death Shall Not Enter the Palace.* He also fantasized U.S. acceptance and recognition of Puerto Rican indigenous culture in the drama *Juan Bobo and the Lady of the Occident.* Marqués prescribed radical solutions for social ills and had to suffer the alienation of a public that was little prepared for such measures. Neither play was ever produced.

Despite censorship, Marqués continues to work, motivated by a sure vision of his country's plight. To this he adds a concern with the crises of the modern epoch — man's solitude, lack of communication with others, his egotistical instinct that overrides love — in such works as *El apartamiento (The Apartment,* 1964), *Carnaval afuera, carnaval adentro (Carnival Outside, Carnival Inside)*[3], and his recent novel *La mirada (The Glance,* 1976). His horrified reaction to war informs the drama *Sacrificio en el Monte Moriah (Sacrifice on Mount Moriah,* 1969) and the sermon *Vía crucis del hombre puertorriqueño (The Puerto Rican's Way of the Cross),* which Marqués read on Palm Sunday 1970 in front of the prison where his son Raúl spent twenty-four hours for refusing to fight with the United States armed forces in Vietnam.

Acclaimed for his literary genius, Marqués also knows the alienation of the idealist who wants more for his fellow men than they want for themselves. Marqués sees his world as tragic and absurd. And by means of literature, he attempts to rectify this situation. Convinced that literature must be more than ornamental, he continues in the face of all obstacles to carry out the vow made in 1944 in *Peregrinación (Pilgrimage)* for his land and for mankind:

> I do not sing of your future
> nor do I offer you the emerald
> of hopes which do not exist;
> I give you harsh words
> that are engraved on your tomb
> cold . . . rigid . . .
> without beauty or poetry.
>
> (yo no canto tu futuro
> ni te ofrezco la esmeralda
> de esperanzas que no existen;
> yo te doy palabras duras
> que se graban en tu tumba
> frías . . . yertas . . .
> sin bellezas ni poesía.)[4]

CHAPTER 2

Marqués' First Novel:
The Eve of Manhood

M ARQUÉS' novel *La víspera del hombre* (*The Eve of Manhood*, 1957) captures the era of Marqués' childhood and adolescence.[1] We witness the social events of the day through the eyes of the young protagonist Pirulo, as we follow his political, physical, and emotional maturation. It seems likely that Pirulo's responses to his environment parallel those formulated by the young Marqués. This identification of author with character depends on the instinct to resist the imposition of ideas and social structures that threaten the very existence of a Puerto Rican identity. Since the novel reflects Puerto Rico's history of dependency, and Marqués-Pirulo's reaction to this history, we shall discuss at some length Pirulo's political maturation.

I *Pirulo's Political Maturation*

As the novel opens, Pirulo stands before the sea in the coastal zone of Carrizal. A lengthy flashback, covering fourteen chapters, recalls the events that have caused him to leave his home on a coffee plantation in the mountains near Lares and emigrate to the coast. Marqués recounts the social and economic factors: The North American occupation of Puerto Rico after 1898 had altered the island's economy, largely by giving priority to sugar cultivation. This prompted the devaluation of coffee production and compelled owners of coffee plantations to sell their property. Tomás Blanco, in his *Prontuario histórico de Puerto Rico* (*Historical Resume of Puerto Rico*), tells us that coffee plantations, owned by small proprietors, had provided employment to many unskilled laborers or *peónes*. Coffee production required no sophisticated, expensive

20

machinery; sugar cultivation, involving huge sums of capital and machinery valued at millions of dollars, fostered the concentration of land in the hands of a few (generally foreign and absentee) corporations.[2] Marqués' novel shows how this economic development devastates a single social unit — Pirulo's family. When Don Rafa, owner of San Isidro, decides to sell the coffee plantation, Pirulo's *peón* stepfather despairs. Turning to drink, he laments his difficult life and dangerously wields his machete. He sells the possesions given to Pirulo's mother after the sale of San Isidro and uses the money to buy liquor.

The economic crisis is reflected in the disruption of Pirulo's sense of identity. Change undermines the security he had felt on the coffee plantation, where he was surrounded by nature and protected by his patron (*padrino*) Don Rafa.[3] Pirulo reproaches Don Rafa for selling San Isidro; Don Rafa responds with a cynical lesson: "You are more than right. No one has the right to sell the land...: But man does not always live according to what is right" ("Te sobra razón. Nadie tiene derecho de vender la tierra...: Pero el hombre no siempre vive de acuerdo al derecho" [p. 29].) Economic, not humanistic, values prevail. In a context of economic turmoil, Pirulo is exposed not only to the despair of his *peón* stepfather, but also to the rational businesslike considerations of the owner.

Faced with the sale of the coffee plantation and the physical destruction of San Isidro in the hurricane of San Felipe (1928), Pirulo eventually leaves for Carrizal. In this coastal zone, the absence of the familiar strikes him: instead of coffee cultivation or banana groves, he finds only stretches of grasslands. Perplexed by options for the future, Pirulo's emotional needs dictate the choice of continued security with Don Rafa, who also owns an estate in Carrizal. Carrizal becomes the only point of orientation — a link between the familiar past and the impenetrable future.

On his way to Carrizal, Pirulo considers other vocations, realizing the *peón's* precarious position in the economy:

Unskilled laborer? OK. But he could also learn a trade. He liked mechanics. He had always helped repair the husking machines. And if not mechanics, something else. Something that he could do with joy. Without hatred. Without resentment. Without temptation to destroy. Something which would convert him into a happy man, and not a bitter man like his stepfather.

(¿Peón? Bueno. Pero también podía aprender un oficio. Le gustaba la mecánica. Había ayudado siempre a componer las máquinas de descascarar. Y si no mecánica, otra cosa. Algo que pudiese hacerse con alegría. Sin odio. Sin resentimientos. Sin tentaciones de destrucción. Algo que le convirtiese en un hombre feliz, no en un amargado como el padrastro [p. 79].)

His stepfather's bitterness instills in Pirulo not resignation, but rather rebellion against the social structure that inspired that bitterness. He becomes increasingly aware of the need for social mobility, and when the truck driver who gives him a ride to Carrizal asks Pirulo about his future plans — "And what are you going to do? Hire yourself out as a servant?" ("¿Y qué vas a hacer? ¿A alquilarte de sirviente?") — Pirulo responds, "I will not serve anyone as a servant." ("Yo no le sirvo de sirviente a nadie" [pp. 81–82].) Pirulo's spirit of resistance is set in relief here, contrasted to the reaction of the truck driver, who breaks into peals of laughter, and then states in a more serious tone that all men like himself and Pirulo are servants in this world, though some do not realize this. He advises Pirulo that joining the Socialist party is the only opportunity to avoid becoming a servant in this world. When Pirulo, grateful for the food and transportation, tells the truck driver that he is a good person, the man shouts, "Imbecile!... In this world there are no good people. If from now on you begin to believe that there are, you are lost" ("¡Imbécil!... En este mundo no hay buenas personas. Si empiezas a pensar desde ahora que las hay, estás perdido" [p. 83]).

But Pirulo refuses to share the bitterness of either his stepfather or this truck driver. Carrizal provides security for the moment, but beyond Carrizal is a vast world: "with the immense blue of the sea as a horizon without limits to his desires for liberty" ("un mundo abierto y franco con la inmensidad azul del mar como horizonte sin límites a sus ansias de libertad" [p. 85]).

Before reaching Carrizal, Pirulo learns about Puerto Rican history from Marcela, a mysterious woman who at one time had sold medicinal plants and herbs in town, while her husband — a Negro — worked on the estate of Don Rodrigo Iturregui. Rumor holds the two guilty of witchcraft, claiming that one of Marcela's spells was tormenting Don Rodrigo. When her lover is fatally shot, Marcela tries to hurl herself from a mountain peak. A worker prevents her suicide, but it is clear that Marcela has lost all reason. The estate is sold; the waters into which her lover's body is thrown are called "the Pond of the Princess" ("la Poza de la Princesa" [p. 59]) and are thought to be inhabited by Indian spirits. Marcela keeps a vigil to the Indian gods Yuquiyú and Jurakán, offering litanies and lighting candles to them. She claims to be a descendant of the men who first fought for liberty in Puerto Rico. Through this exotic woman, Pirulo absorbs the spirit of individualism and the strength of the Indian resistance to the Spaniards — the first foreign invaders of Puerto Rico. Marcela represents an alternative to his family's prosaic, resigned existence.

Marcela reveals to Pirulo an Indian legend dating from the time of the Spanish conquest, a legend that parallels her own life to a curious degree: an Indian princess, Anaiboa, loves one of her father's warriors but, as a condition of a peace treaty, must marry the Spanish captain Don Rodrigo. The princess and her lover "Manicato" flee to the mountain, where they dedicate themselves to their love under the stars. The romance intensifies as the enemy encroaches on the lovers' ideal world. Dreams of the pre-Columbian world serve as a nostalgic, sad prelude to the murder: Don Rodrigo kills his sleeping Indian rival in cold blood. Frightened, the princess flees, but does not overlook the sight of her lover's body flung into the water under a blood-red moon. Resisting Don Rodrigo, the foreign assassin of the Indian and destroyer of all the Indian represents, she climbs to a rock overlooking the water and commits suicide. As the princess performs her act of defiance, the Spaniards hear a single word in Indian dialect — *taíno* — which may be understood both as a curse on their race and as a prophecy. The legend ends with the romantic union of the lovers in the world beyond: "The Indian chief's daughter was reunited with the Indian warrior, never again to be seen by a white man" ("La hija del cacique se había ya reunido con el guerrero indio y ningún hombre blanco la vería jamás" [p. 49]). Pirulo identifies with this heroic resistance: "What a pity not to have lived in that epoch of Indians and Spaniards! He would have been an Indian, of course. To defend the Indian chief's daughter" ("¡Qué lástima no haber vivido en aquella época de indios y españoles! El habría sido indio, desde luego. Para defender a la hija del cacique" [p. 51]).

As Marqués develops his protagonist in the first fourteen chapters, Pirulo's eyes are increasingly opened to the political implications of the Spanish and North American invasions that molded Puerto Rico's economy and history. Pirulo's stepfather fills in background information about the island's resistance to Spanish domination; he explains how "The Cry of Lares" ("El Grito de Lares," 1868) is commemorated on the town square: "The stepfather had explained to him that many, many years ago there was a revolution in Lares. It was a war against the government of Spain to make Puerto Rico free. But Puerto Rico was not freed because the revolution came to nothing."[4] ("El padrastro le había explicado que hacía muchos, muchos años, había habido una revolución en Lares. Era como una guerra contra el gobierno de España para hacer a Puerto Rico libre. Pero Puerto Rico no fue libre porque la revolución se quedó en nada.") Pirulo perceives his stepfather's scorn for any effort to resist Spanish rule: " 'Instead of fighting, the Puerto Ricans shouted,' " the stepfather had said laughing savagely. " 'That's why they call it the Cry of Lares' " (" — En vez de pelear, los puertorriqueños gritaron — había dicho el padrastro riendo salvajemente —. Por eso lo llaman el Grito de Lares" [pp. 35–36]).

Pirulo relates the earlier movement for liberation from Spain to the present movement for liberation from the United States. At the celebration in the square, the Lares insurrection is invoked to incite action toward autonomy. The speaker at the celebration is Albizu Campos, who in 1930 was elected president of the nationalist party, which supported independence; he stresses the continuity of the revolutionary struggle, stating that although the adversary was now the United States, Puerto Rico was still fighting for liberty. At the emotional celebration, Albizu tearfully embraces "The daughter of the Caribbean," who has recited verses and presented Albizu with a silk flag; the people shout "Long live the republic! Long live liberty!" ("¡Viva la república! ¡Viva la libertad!" [p. 36]). The drama does not move Pirulo's stepfather, but it does interest Pirulo, although the boy does not fully understand its meaning. He begins to discern the conflict between an independent Puerto Rico and a Puerto Rico under the United States' flag, but cannot yet deal with the question of affiliation. At this point he only muses on his new knowledge.

The first fourteen chapters provide us with a view of Pirulo's political and social consciousness raising. Only after reaching Carrizal does he begin to formulate definite political convictions. A school experience shapes Pirulo's judgement. When his schoolmates salute the American flag, Pirulo's poor English allows him to capture only three words: republic, justice, and liberty. Pirulo remembers that Albizu Campos also endorsed these ideals:

Did not Albizu also speak of the republic, of justice and liberty, in the square at Lares? Then why didn't the police like him? Or at any rate, why did the police allow these ideas to be spoken of here in the school? Now Pirulo was really confused.

(¿No era también de la república, de la justicia y de la libertad de lo que hablaba el señor trigueño que llamaban Albizu, allá en la plaza de Lares? ¿Por qué entonces la policía no lo quería? O en todo caso, ¿por qué la policía permitía que se hablara de eso aquí en la escuela? Pirulo estaba ahora realmente confundido [p. 126].)

The principal observes that Pirulo does not join the others in the salute. This "Miss," a woman completely imbued with the North American way of life, fully colonized and anxious to colonize others, a woman whose office wall is decorated with the American flag and a picture of George Washington,[5] fiercely confronts Pirulo, "Are you or are you not an American citizen?" ("¿Eres o no eres ciudadano americano?"); Pirulo answers simply, "I am from Lares." ("Yo soy de Lares" [p. 127]). He does not grasp the concept of loyalty to an entity further removed than this region. Failing to understand this, the principal scorns Pirulo's rural background: "You must be a stupid mountain peasant! But don't you know, animal, that we are all Americans?" ("¡Jíbaro bruto de la montaña tenías que ser! ¿Pero no sabes, animal, que todos somos americanos?" [p. 127]). Pirulo resists her and stubbornly repeats that he was born in Lares. When the principal later attacks him with brute force, Marqués tells us that Pirulo, in his stupor, does not even try to defend himself, until another blow leaves him stunned. His plans for revenge are frustrated; his retaliation can only be verbal. He shouts: "Neither you nor anyone else can make me an American if I don't want to be one!" ("¡Si yo no quiero, ni usted ni nadie me puede hacer americano!" [p. 128]). Without fully understanding what it is to be an American, Pirulo establishes his commitment to Puerto Rico, rejecting the United States. He is still forced to say the pledge in English, but when he can get away with it, he curses the principal instead of reciting the pledge.

Pirulo continues his routine existence in Carrizal, attending school and helping his aunt and uncle who are *peónes* on the estate. He remains sensitive to the injustices inflicted on Puerto Ricans by Americans or by his Americanized countrymen. He bitterly resents being forced to give charity to the widow of an American school inspector killed by a nationalist in San Juan. Pirulo feels that he is not guilty of murder and objects to the fact that although the widow receives compensation from the government, he is nevertheless ordered by the commissioner of education to give money: "And he thought bitterly that when all the money taken from all the poor children of all the schools was put together, the American widow would be a millionaire. But he would remain the same." ("Y pensó con amargura que cuando se juntaran todas las pesetas de todos los niños pobres de todas las escuelas, la americana aquella iba a ser millonaria. Pero él seguiría igual" [p. 131]).

Pirulo's reaction against American domination is based largely on economic factors: he has seen his secure world of the coffee plantation destroyed and has witnessed the bitterness of his *peón* stepfather toward economic changes produced by North American interest in sugar over coffee. But his resistance is also politically motivated against a government that clearly stresses the rights of Americans. Gordon K. Lewis tells us of this epoch: "Although there was nothing in the provisions of the Organic Acts to debar the appointment of a local candidate, all the Governors until 1947 . . . were Americans, with the single exception of Governor Piñero in 1946." By underlining Pirulo's limited knowledge of English in the school episode, Marqués raises the issue of American educational policies in Puerto Rico that, after 1900:

amounted in reality to the inculcation of "Americanism," the extension of the school system and the teaching of English.

· ·

The use of English as a medium of instruction meant, as the 1925 Survey Commission pointed out, not only that children did not remain long enough in school to obtain a real mastery of English, but also that all other subjects suffered, both on account of the priority of English in the curriculum and on account of the transmission of those subjects in a broken and formalized English on the part of inadequately prepared teachers. . . . The pedagogical problem became, frankly enough, a political issue. To criticize the policy was to expose oneself to charges of sedition and "un-American" attitudes.[6]

Pirulo increasingly values the "un-American" way. With this orientation, he interacts with Raúl, Don Rafa's young grandson, who has been studying in the United States. Raúl is fast becoming a lettered man of the United States, ready to elevate everything to universal terms. He is not interested in his country's folklore, which is the pride of the *jíbaros* (peasants); he prefers to talk about Boccaccio's *Decameron* as the source of such folklore. Marqués' portrait of Raúl anticipates Enrique Laguerre's opposition to the Puerto Rican university mentality in the early 1950s. Enrique Laguerre, in his *Pulso de Puerto Rico* (*Pulse of Puerto Rico*), laments the fact that Puerto Rican university students and leaders, even if they don't emigrate as Raúl did, still prefer to concentrate on foreign culture before first understanding what constitutes their own country, its folklore, or any other aspect of its heritage. Laguerre asks, "Is our University truly informed of our collective realities?" ("¿Está nuestra Universidad verdaderamente enterada de nuestras realidades colectivas?"). He denounces "that desire to flee, away from our realities—..." ("esa ansia de fuga, fuera de nuestras realidades—...") and urges appreciation of regional culture as a point of departure for understanding the rest of the world: "looking outside with the spirit focused on what is inside the country" ("el mirar, sí, hacia afuera con el espíritu puesto en lo de adentro").[7] Similarly, Marqués criticizes the "universalism" that arose after World War II in his essay "Un autor, un intríngulis y una obra" ("An author, a Plot and a Work"):

By means of this supposed "universalism" — which had its most ridiculous expression this year (1953) when the University of Puerto Rico dropped from its program of studies the course on Puerto Rican literature as an academic requirement — not only is the study of what is indigenous avoided, but it is openly attacked as a manifestation of a lack of culture, of mere provincialism.

(Mediante este pretendido "universalismo" — que tuvo su expresión más ridícula este año de gracia de 1953 al eliminar la Universidad de Puerto Rico de su programa de estudios, como requisito académico, el curso de Literatura Puertorriqueña — , no sólo se evade el estudio de lo autóctono, sino que se ataca abiertamente como manifestación de incultura, de mero provincialismo [*Ensayos,* p. 19]).

Raúl tells Pirulo that he wants fame and glory through politics: "One can be a great writer, or a great musician, for example. But there is an easier route: politics" ("Se puede ser un gran escritor, o un gran músico, por ejemplo. Pero hay un camino más fácil: la política" [p. 250]). Raúl envisions gradual change until eventually a Puerto Rican will govern the island. Pirulo does not wish governorship for Raúl and argues that it would be better to be president of the republic. He believes in the future liberation of Puerto Rico and in the establishment of a republic under the presidency of Albizu Campos. Raúl espouses political and economic dependency on the United States, insisting that Puerto Rico will never be free. Were she free, he says, her people would starve. Pirulo is amazed at the idea Raúl has evidently learned in the United States and at his justification of such an idea. When Raúl asks whether Pirulo would vote for him if he ran for governor, Pirulo replies, "I would never vote for you. . . . Nor will I vote for any politician who does not believe in liberty for my people" ("Pues no votaré nunca por ti. . . . Ni votaré por ningún político que no crea en la libertad de mi gente" [p. 251]). Raúl disdainfully calls Pirulo a nationalist. Pirulo replies with sincerity: "I don't know if I am a nationalist. But I've read that in India, Gandhi is starving himself to death for the liberty of his people. And no one calls him crazy" ("Yo no sé si soy nacionalista. Pero he leído que en la India, Gandhi se muere de hambre por la libertad de los suyos. Y nadie le llama loco" [p. 251]). When Raúl shouts at him that he does not understand anything, Pirulo responds that he *feels;* even if there were no Albizu in Puerto Rico or Gandhi in India, he would feel exactly the same way. And he only understands what he feels.

II   *Love for the Land*

Pirulo knows that he will always identify with those who seek liberty. He has seen how poverty embittered his stepfather and martyred his mother. He has observed how economic changes undermined the humanistic views of Don Rafa. Pirulo understands the limitations of the rural population — their resignation to poverty and their inertia — yet he remains optimistic about the possibility of changing the world by shaping the attitudes of its inhabitants. His accumulated experiences compel him to resist the status quo that Raúl tries so fervently to protect. He feels obliged to keep watch over those who, like Raúl, are capable of selling themselves for any price. Standing on an elevated rock overlooking the sea, Raúl looks toward the United States and Pirulo toward Puerto Rico. Raúl accepts the orientation toward society passed down by his family. He and his widowed mother Doña Isabel increasingly identify with the United States, leaving the land and becoming urbanized. Despite Don Rafa's affinity to the land, he sells his property. Committed to progress, he buys an American-made Buick, despite his business associate's condemnation of "those accursed American machines" ("esas condenadas máquinas 'americanas' " [p. 210]). This interpretation of "progress" is part of Raúl's primary socialization. Pirulo, on the other hand, disdains urbanization and North Americanization; he prefers the country, where "the environment masked the misery of the flesh, the poverty of the clothing," ("el ambiente disimulaba la miseria de las carnes, la pobreza de las ropas,...); where "the blue of the sky was very high. And the green vegetation succeeded in putting into sharper relief the picturesque identification of man and his environment" (el azul del cielo estaba muy alto. Y el verde de la vegetación sólo lograba hacer resaltar más esta identificación pictórica del hombre y su medio" [p. 201]). He is drawn to the wholesome spirit of Félix, the black man whose natural poetic sentiment contrasts with Don Rafa's rational approach. Pirulo may combine the rational and spiritual in his own life, but he is still entranced by Félix's tales of the sea, of the ships that pass in the distance, and of the pirate Cofresí who buried a treasure beneath the sea's rock. Pirulo values moments of solitude, when he feels close to the land and the sea. Here he finds the security and the identity that his political context does not provide. He appreciates "the rhythmic ceremony of the waves which break against the rocks..." and savors the "bittersweet flavor of grapes on the beach. ...salt, dew, sand." ("el ceremonial rítmico de las olas al romper sobre las rocas:...," "el sabor agridulce de las uvas playeras. ...sal, rocío y arena" [p. 130]). He experiences a more intense union with nature in an erotic involvement with Félix's daughter Lita. The love scene is set on the sands near the sea.

Marqués reflects in the character Pirulo his own preference for the country over the city,[8] a preference that is marked in the novel. Marqués deplores the urbanization of an essentially agricultural country. His account of the city of Arecibo features foul odors, filth, and prostitution:

But here, in the urban narrowness, there was no fusion between nature and man. Perhaps because here nature existed only as a human expression, and not by itself. Perhaps because the city, man's creation, brought to the surface the dirtiness, the baseness, the miserable state of its maker. In Arecibo the *jíbaro's* poverty was stripped naked: anemia on the faces, threadbare clothes, calloused hands, feet without shoes. In Carrizal a bare foot sinking into the sand was a natural and intimate fusion between man and the land.

(Pero aquí, en la estrechez urbana, no había fusión de la naturaleza y el hombre. Quizá porque aquí la naturaleza existía sólo como expresión humana, y no por sí misma. Quizá porque la ciudad, hechura del hombre, sacaba a la superficie todo lo sucio, lo bajo, lo miserable de su hacedor. En Arecibo la pobreza del jíbaro se mostraba desnuda: la anemia en los rostros, las ropas raídas, las manos curtidas, los pies sin zapatos. En Carrizal un pie descalzo hundiéndose en la arena era una fusión natural e íntima del hombre y la tierra [p. 202].)

Marqués traces the abandonment of the land over four generations of Don Rafa's family: Don Francisco Abreu, Don Rafa's father-in-law, came to America from the Canary Islands to make his fortune by working the land; Don Rafa sells the land; his children and grandchildren become increasingly urbanized. Don Rafa exists between two worlds. He is a kind and just plantation owner whose efforts to provide help and justice for his employees is institutionalized in a weekly payday routine: as each worker personally receives his wages from Don Rafa, the patron listens to his problems and dispenses advice (Chapter XXIV). On one occasion, Don Rafa and his wife Doña Irene offer moral support to Félix's agonized wife when the man disappears in the swamp.

Don Rafa's wish for Pirulo to study the history of his own country is a form of resistance to Americanization. But his realization that his country is being sold out to the Americans is mixed with curious acceptance of this "progress" and with the wish to acquire American products. His willingness to move with the times contrasts with his wife's resistance to modernity. She sits with the peasants in the evening to shell green pigeon peas (*gandules*) and to hear the stories that accompany the gathering. The peasants reject the use of machinery that would facilitate the shelling process; Marqués insists that some customs should never give way to progress.

III *Physical and Emotional Maturation*

Pirulo's comprehension of the island's troubled political situation parallels his early exposure to a troubled family situation. Poverty causes his mother's martyrdom and forces his disgruntled stepfather to think of Pirulo as an economic burden. The man tells Pirulo's mother: "Listen, Juana, if we don't get more money for this boy, it is not worth having him around" ("Oye, Juana, si no sacamos más chavos por este muchacho no vale la pena tenerlo" [p. 11]). The stepfather's drunken fury terrifies the young boy. Pirulo soon discovers that poverty is not the only cause of unhappiness, for Don Rafa's well-to-do family also seems miserable. The only truly content individual is Pirulo's innocent younger brother. Observing him at play one day, Pirulo asks his mother, "Do you believe that some day I will be as happy as the baby?" ("¿Tú crees que yo algún día pueda estar tan contento como el nene?" [p. 23]). But discontent seems to be the order of the day. Only in Carrizal does Pirulo meet a truly warm person; Félix is the first person in Pirulo's experience who can really laugh:

The peals of laughter sounded deep, as if they came from deep within, as if they flowed from a fountain of rich, lavish, inexhaustible life. Suddenly Pirulo realized that he had never heard anyone laugh in this way.... Laughing was not a custom of the people who had formed his world.

(Las carcajadas sonaban hondas, como si salieran de muy adentro, como si brotaran de una fuente de vida rica, pródiga, inagotable. De pronto Pirulo se dio cuenta de que jamás había oído a nadie reír de ese modo.... Reír no era hábito de la gente que había formado su mundo [p. 93].)

Carrizal becomes a turning point for Pirulo, as hints of joy begin to fill his life. He experiences more intimacy with Don Rafa. Along with his new sense of national history, he acquires a sense of family history when he learns about the life of Don Abreu. He takes pride in mastering elements of his environment, such as Don Rafa's horse, and later his coach and car. At first terrified of the sea, Pirulo soon learns to love it. His coming of age is not only spiritual — he falls in love with Félix's daughter. Marqués portrays Pirulo's possession of Lita poetically: his sensation of being at one with nature — the clouds, sky, sun, sands, sea — evolves into his oneness with Lita: "Water-Pirulo, land-Pirulo, Lita-Pirulo." ("agua-Pirulo, tierra-Pirulo, Lita-Pirulo" [p. 222]).

Pirulo's new life is not without sorrow. He identifies with the sorrows of others: the cancerous face of a local character named Monchín del Alma; the tragedy of a young peasant girl who runs off with a married man and who then dies in childbirth. Pirulo's own joys are bittersweet. His love for Lita is tinged with jealousy when Raúl becomes a rival for the girl's affections. Pirulo's jealousy intensifies until he attempts to push Raúl into the sea. The thrill of possessing Lita is transformed into grotesque tragedy when Lita becomes pregnant.[9] Her dishonored father Félix disappears into the swamp and apparently commits suicide; her enraged stepmother murders the girl with her husband's machete. Lita is likened symbolically to a heron (*garza*), a bird whose fate is always tragic. Embracing Lita's blood-stained body near the sea, Pirulo feels a kinship with all the people who have experienced the pain, anxiety, and desperation of living. Pirulo's search for joy seems to have ended in the blackest pessimism.

But Marqués exposes Pirulo to one more shattering experience to initiate him to the depths of life's joy. Learning that he is in fact Don Rafa's son, Pirulo attempts suicide, but is stopped by what appears to be the voice of the dead Félix telling him that he must live. Félix, whom Pirulo had loved and hurt, guides Pirulo into manhood. Marqués ends his novel with the image of the sun, the traditional symbol of life: "tomorrow, in the east, the sun would rise again" ("mañana, por oriente, saldría de nuevo el sol" [p. 287]). With the dawn of a new day, Pirulo's coming of age is complete — politically, physically, and emotionally.

Marqués portrays Pirulo's suspension between childhood and manhood with reasonable credibility. Pirulo plays games, fantasizes, and dreams. His naïveté expresses itself rather humorously when Pirulo hears Albizu Campos' reference to Puerto Rico's "war" against the United States, but cannot think in terms of ideological combat: "Pirulo was surprised that Puerto Rico was at war and that shots were not heard in Lares. But perhaps the war was on the coast and the shots did not reach the mountain." ("A Pirulo le sorprendía que Puerto Rico estuviese en guerra y que en Lares no se oyeran los tiros. Pero quizá la guerra era en la costa y los tiros no llegaban a la montaña" [p. 36].)

In some respects, however, Pirulo's role as a mouthpiece for Marqués makes him seem too mature and too politically oriented for his age. Marqués sacrifices verisimilitude of characterization for the sake of political doctrine. When Pirulo first comes to his aunt and uncle's house in Carrizal, Don Rafa asks him why he chose to leave San Isidro. Pirulo replies, "I don't want to depend on anyone" ("No quiero depender de nadie" [p. 103]). He adds that he would be happy to work the land if only he owned it himself. This articulation of the author's reaction against dependency on the United States and against the usurpation of land by the self-interested North Americans seem premature in Pirulo.

IV *Style*

Marqués' novel makes a single life a microcosm of the society in which he lives. Pirulo must accept that his pleasure with Lita has drastic consequences for her and her family. The message is clear: Puerto Rico must also face the consequences of its indulgence in materialistic pleasure and the fruits of "progress." Marqués parallels Pirulo's illegitimacy with that of his island. Learning that he is Don Rafa's bastard son, Pirulo muses on "his nation, as he, a bastard ... his nation in shadows" ("su pueblo, como él, bastardo, ... su pueblo en sombras" [p. 285]).

Marqués makes frequent use of parallelisms to illustrate the cyclical nature of history and the deeply rooted spiritual qualities that motivate men who live in different epochs. Don Abreu's tremendous will and spirit of resistance reappears two generations later in Pirulo. The growing complexity of Don Abreu's life stemming from his marriage parallels the change in Pirulo's life after his involvement with Lita. Marqués also sets the Indians' memories of the pre-Columbian world against Pirulo's dreams of life before the sale of San Isidro. Two worlds, two epochs, both involve the violation of an ordered existence by an outside force.

Marqués frequently makes symbolic use of nature in the novel. He portrays the instinct to resist invasion in the natural sphere, in order to urge resistance in the political sphere. Pirulo watches a bird of prey attack another bird — the *pitirre*. The *pitirre* successfully wards off the attack: "And upon the tallest palm tree ... the *pitirre* erected his pride, once again owner and master of his domain" ("Y sobre la palma real más alta, ... volvió el pitirre a enhiestar su orgullo, dueño y señor una vez más de sus dominios" [p. 65]). The sea resists man's intrusion into its domain: Pirulo, standing before the sea, is seized with terror as he watches the waves become more furious and overwhelming, "As if the presence of the intruder aroused the implacable ire of the monster" ("Como si la presencia del intruso excitara la ira implacable del monstruo" [p. 118]).

Marqués also uses nature to symbolize the dangers of resistance. Floating on a raft, Pirulo recalls the inspiring resistance of the Indian princess Anaiboa. Suddenly the raft becomes loosened from its mooring and is nearly destroyed by a rushing current, a waterfall, and dangerous rocks. The symbolic manipulation of the raft is clear: at first it is moored, although its slight movement gives the illusion of liberty. When the raft breaks its tie with the shore, its rider is endangered. Attempting to escape his dismal existence — to seek liberty — Pirulo faces other dangers. When he reaches Carrizal, with scratched feet and torn clothing, he is threatened by pursuing dogs and later falls from the tree in which he sought refuge.

The character Lita is associated in the novel with a heron, a bird whose fate is always tragic. Marqués uses the symbol of the bird to create suspense through anticipation — a technique typical of his drama. In Chapter XVII, Pirulo sees a beautiful heron moving about strangely in the infested waters of the swamp. When he learns that Raúl often hunts wild ducks in the swamp, Pirulo begins to imagine the heron's plumage stained with blood and resolves to protect the heron from Raúl. In Chapter XIX, Pirulo glimpses Lita spying on him near the swamp. When she runs off, he thinks of her as a snow-white heron taking flight. The image anticipates Lita's future: her whiteness, her purity, will be stained by the social condemnation when she loses her virginity and becomes pregnant. She is killed not by Raúl, but by her crazed stepmother; ironically, it is Pirulo himself who is indirectly responsible for her death.

Marqués also uses anticipation to suggest Pirulo's true identity. He hints at Pirulo's relationship to Don Rafa early in the work: In Chapter II, Doña Irene's voice trembles when she speaks to Pirulo, and the servants smile maliciously. Pirulo's eyes are also described as being as gray as Don Rafa's.

Along with anticipating events, Marqués makes use of the flashback technique. Pirulo's meditation on the old family mansion in Carrizal (and later the portrait of Don Abreu) is almost cinematographic in effect. Of the two, the best developed flashback is the initial one. The present is linked to the past with the theme of isolation. Pirulo's sense of abandonment near the sea in Carrizal is a continuation of the emotional isolation and insecurity of his family life in Lares.

The Eve of Manhood won the 1962 Iberian American prize for the novel from the William Faulkner Foundation. Many of the stylistic tools developed by Marqués in this novel are also found in his short stories and dramas.

CHAPTER 3

Poetry: Pilgrimage

A T age twenty-five, Marqués wrote *Peregrinación* (1944), impassioned verse that approaches such large questions as the nature of war, love, illusion and reality, and Marqués' native land. The book is divided into five sections: Marqués' pilgrimage takes him into war, to the land, to the moon, to love, and finally to the shadows of life. The various sections are united by the presence of Marqués — the "Pilgrim" ("El peregrino") — who describes himself as alive, vigilant, a body whose perception is facilitated by one hundred pupils, a nerve with perpetual insomnia, supersensitive viscera, an awakened voice,[1] a man alert to the social and existential problems of his day — an alertness that he hopes will be infused in his countrymen.

I *To War*

In the first segment "To War" ("A la guerra"), Marqués' basic hatred of war finds expression in two poems. In "Campamento" ("Encampment"), the environment is dusty, gray, bloody, filled with cries, tombs, mummies. The encampment becomes a "waiting room for death" ("Antesala de la muerte"), a "cemetery of live men" ("Cementerio de hombres vivos" [p. 10]). In the poem "Prisionero en la selva" ("Prisoner in the Jungle"), Marqués deplores man's imprisonment in the jungle of war where the "reptiles" of hatred, untruth, and cynicism reign — where death comes before one even gets to know life.

Marqués' hatred of war makes him especially resentful of the consequences of World War II for his land. Historically, the island's socioeconomic reorganization was preempted by the routines of war.[2] When the United States entered the war in 1941, the Puerto Rican Regiment 65 was sent to fight in Europe. In "Oración roja en la muerte del labriego" ("Red Prayer upon the Peasant's Death"), Marqués anticipates the peasant's death in his description of nature: the bloody waterfall and moon, and the ceiba tree that seems to produce muffled complaints from beyond the tomb. Marqués speaks of a farmer in the armed forces, lamenting the draftee's loss of his wholesome existence and his pure relationship with the land:

> It is the war of the fierce beasts
> in the jungle of the sea-world.
> And they took you off to war...
> And you were nostalgic for the poverty
> of your ranch,
> the murmuring waterfall,
> the mountain adorned by the moon,
> and the hundred-year-old ceiba tree....
>
> (Es la guerra de las fieras
> en la selva del mar-mundo.
> Y a la guerra te llevaron...
> Y añorabas la pobreza
> de tu rancho,
> la cascada rumorosa,
> la montaña engalanada por la luna,
> y la ceiba centenaria... [p. 12].)

The peasant is told that he must fight for his country; Marqués insists that the peasant fights not for his nation, but for the sake of those who have no commitment to his land. Imagining the peasant's death, Marqués even describes the man's grief as pleasure in comparison with his anguish over the injustices perpetrated against his nation.

II   To the Land

In the section "To the Land" ("A la tierra"), Marqués points out another traumatic consequence of Puerto Rico's dependency on the United States, already seen in *The Eve of Manhood:* the devaluation of coffee cultivation and the supremacy of the North American interest in sugar cultivation. Marqués treats this theme in "Vida, pasión y muerte de mi río isleño" ("Life, Passion and Death of my Island River"). Born in the mountains, the river is at first free from sorrow. As it flows through coffee plantations, the peasant's sweat flows into its waters. The river flows on to the plain, where the blood of the sugar plantations stains its water. Before the river even reaches this destination, Marqués describes the cry of the dogs — a traditional symbol of death — passing through the veins of the river.

In the poem "Canción cínica para no ser cantada" ("A Cynical Song not to be Sung"), Marqués thinks of his land first as a mother who gave him the "milk of hope" ("leche de esperanzas" [p. 21]) and then identifies with her as a son and lover:

> In the waters of the Caribbean
> incest was liturgy!
> I pressed the mountains-breasts
> rooted with palm trees,
> and I bit the lips-rocks
> in the mouth of San Juan.

> (¡En las aguas del Caribe
> el incesto fué liturgia!
> Y apreté los montes-senos
> enraizados de palmeras,
> y mordí los labios-piedras
> en la Boca de San Juan [p. 22].)

His land, violated by the invader, is no longer virginal:

> Your flesh is no longer your flesh,
> it was bought
> by the beasts
> who invaded your entrails.
> You deceived me land-female,
> you were not a virgin
> nor were you mine...!

> (Ya tu carne no es tu carne,
> fue comprada
> por las fieras
> que invadieron tus entrañas.
> ¡Me engañaste tierra-hembra,
> no eras virgen
> ni eras mía...! [p. 23].)

In view of this, Marqués vows revenge:

> But one day,

I swear to you by the flesh
of your breasts,
I will avenge the infamous insult.

(Pero un día,
te lo juro por la carne
de tus senos,
vengaré la afrenta infame [p.
24].)

He envisions a day when the land will entice the invader with its
sensuality (its dark flesh sprinkled with dew; its mane of coffee
unbraided near the river, scented by the mountain):

The master will come
for your flesh. . .
and that day
inflamed with lust,
along the material of your skirt
will flow the black blood
of the robber-carnivore-lover.
(With the strands of your hair
I will make cords
that will twist his throat)

(Vendrá el amo
por tu carne. . .
Y ese día
encendido de lujuria,
por la tela de tu falda
correrá la sangre negra
del ladrón-chacal-amante.
[Con los hilos de tu pelo
haré cuerdas
que retuerzan su garganta] [pp.
24–25].)

Although the imagery here is basically anatomical, political associations are not lacking. The murder weapon, the hair that will
strangle the master, is appropriately associated with the coffee
plantation whose indigenous crop has taken second place to sugar
cane cultivation. The master's blood will irrigate the land; his death
will allow the land to bloom once again. But the land will also be
black with the hatred and vengeance of the people — voiced by
Marqués.

In this section, Marqués' poems contrast the real with the ideal, a juxtaposition that dominates all of Marqués' literary production. In the poem "Tierra triste" ("Sad Land"), Marqués describes how the land's creative potential has been thwarted: colonization has destroyed completely "the ovaries" of the land: "la colonia te ha extirpado los ovarios" (p. 38). He describes his land's breasts as two dry rivers: "y tus pechos son dos ríos sin sus aguas..." (p. 38). In "El pozo" ("The Pool"), Marqués likens his island to a stagnant pool, which has moss growing over its eye. This poem recalls Antonio Machado's "Las ascuas de un crepúsculo" ("The Embers of Twilight").

The sterility attributed to nature is also reflected in the resigned silence and inertia of its inhabitants. In "El hombre de tierra" ("The Peasant"), Marqués portrays the rural man as an amorphous mass of flesh and death ("masa amorfa / de carne y de muerte"), whose entrails are pierced by two hundred vultures ("Doscientos buitres / le pican la entraña" [p. 29]). The man is a docile beast whose pupils are dead and who is therefore without vision. Marqués wants ideals to penetrate the inert flesh (yo daría... / todo mi esqueleto / por ... / saber que hay sueños / en la carne inerte,..." [p. 30]); in short, he wants the beast to become a man. Becoming a man means undergoing a political consciousness raising, abandoning one's resignation, and becoming concerned with the plight of the land. Marqués serves as the model. In the poem "Paréntesis" ("Parenthesis"), Marqués urges a tree (described as a lover) to bloom in the author's valley; its branches must entwine themselves around his neck, its sap of vitality must be infused into his being lest he turn into a stone of indifference and resignation.[3] Marqués expresses the wish to assume his land's anguish and tragedy in the poem "Un alto en la faena" ("A Halt in the Task"), for in this way he will absolve his own guilt: "¡Mi alma lavará sus culpas / en la triste tragedia de mi tierra!" (p. 41).

III *To the Moon*

Yet in the next section, entitled "The Journey to the Moon" ("A la luna"), we witness a reversal. In a tone reminiscent of Lugones' *Lunaria sentimental (Sentimental Period Between Two New Moons),* Marqués verbalizes the impulse to abandon his moral position — to escape to the moon. Marqués shouts, in "Fuga en tono blanco hacia la luna" ("Flight in White Tone Toward the

Moon"), "Today I return to my poet's castle!" ("¡hoy regreso a
mi castillo de poeta!") and leaves personal and national tragedy
behind him ("En la tierra se ha quedado / mi tragedia..."
[p. 46]). He desires a return to innocence — unstained by sorrow,
blood, tragedy:

> I want clouds that will wash
> the blackness of my stains,
> of the stains that muddied
> the whiteness of my silver dreams!

> (quiero nubes que me laven
> la negrura de mis manchas,
> ¡de estas manchas que enturbiaron
> la blancura de mis sueños argentados! [p. 46].)

However, the hint of disenchantment occurs in "Embrujo de
luna" ("Enchantment of the Moon"):

> I approached quietly...
> I touched your flesh...
> my hand froze
> upon your body
> White silence!

> (Me acerqué quedo...
> toqué tu carne...
> mi mano helóse
> sobre tu cuerpo
> ¡Silencio blanco! [pp. 48–49].)

His beloved is bewitched by a jealous moon. In the poem "Crepúsculo" ("Twilight"), Marqués describes a bull's demise in the
arena. His lover's eyes are fixed upon the heroic bullfighter, leaving
Marqués wounded spiritually, just as the bull is physically
wounded. The seemingly frivolous escape to the moon has clear
social import. Marqués' attempt to find a pure existence divorced
from sorrows leaves him once again in a world of deceit, sorrow,
pain, death. The writer realizes that he is deluding himself when he
deviates from his social role. In his essay "La función del escritor
puertorriqueño en el momento actual" ("The Function of the
Puerto Rican Writer at the Present Moment"), Marqués declares
that the writer's first concern should be aesthetics. Yet his mission
involves an agonizing and interminable search for truth: "And it is

not in starry places where the writer looks for truth, but in Man, in his fellow man, in the society which surrounds him.'' (''Y no es en los espacios siderales donde el escritor busca la verdad sino en el Hombre, en sus semejantes, en la sociedad que le rodea'' [*Ensayos,* p. 221]). The writer can therefore never abandon the reality in which he lives; he must face this reality, and must distill truth from its myriad contradictions.

Returning to the world, Marqués sings briefly of the joys of life, celebrating motherhood (''Maternidad''). He contrasts the silent anticipation with the glorious cry of the child at birth. In the poem ''Confesión'' (''Confession''), the poet expresses his desire to sing of life's beauty and to compose sonnets that for him abound with the taste of almonds and the perfume of gardenias (''sonetos floridos / con sabor a almendras y olor a gardenias'' [p. 63]). Yet he knows that his poetic mission lies elsewhere: his verse can only express the sorrow of life. His words contain the dye of mud, mixed with rocks, shadows, laments.

IV To Life's Shadows

In the final section, Marqués proceeds from a social to an existential stance, verbalizing a pessimistic attitude toward life in general. In ''Sonata de la soledad'' (''Sonata of Loneliness''), the awareness of the poet's loneliness in the context of an absurd world recalls Pablo Neruda's ''Walking Around.''[4] In ''El sueño de las sombras'' (''The Dream of Shadows''), facing the black of night — his dead love, and a grotesque parade of vampires, crows, howling dogs from beyond the tomb — the poet decides that he is the dead man in life. In the poem ''Naufragio'' (''Shipwreck''), the description of a shipwreck suggests another kind of devastation — the metaphysical shipwreck of the soul. The poem ''Ese mar'' (''That Sea'') follows through on this image, depicting the sea as a body that provides no solace, but only dissolves the poet's own soul. In ''Sonata de la soledad,'' (''Sonata of Loneliness'') Marqués views the chaos of his world through a window and chaotically reports what he sees: sobs, tombs, black crosses, hysteria of sick laughter, the flight of teeth from mouths deformed by laughter. He deplores the trappings of the modern world: skyscrapers, heliocopters that chew the herons of the sky, birds that become steel and drink up the gold of the sun, noise, rivers of alcohol-infested blood (pp. 68–69). Marqués retreats from this absurd existence, and in the poem

"Péndulo eterno" ("Eternal Pendulum"), he finds himself faced only with infinity and nothingness.

Marqués infused into his poetry the themes that were later expanded in his drama. The author's abhorrence of war, and of the Puerto Rican commitment to the United States armed forces, recurs years later when he protests the U.S. involvement in Vietnam in the prologue to his drama *Sacrifice on Mount Moriah* (1969) and in the short dramatic piece *The Puerto Rican's Way of the Cross*. He treats the theme of personal guilt for his nation's plight in *The House Without a Clock* (1960), as well as in the famous essay "El puertorriqueño dócil" ("The Docile Puerto Rican"). The problems of the modern world treated in "Sonata of Loneliness" are developed in his drama *Carnival Outside, Carnival Inside* (1960), and the existential isolation of the poem "Eternal Pendulum" becomes the central theme of his drama *The Apartment* (1964).

Marqués is writing in the tradition of many of his countrymen, especially Gautier Benítez, when he repeats the image of his land as a beautiful, innocent woman who loses her freshness, ardor, fertility, when she is raped by the invader. Marqués' imagery is daring: the inhabitants of his island are beasts, his land is a stagnant pool. Borrowing a symbol from the modernists, Marqués describes his land as an orphan swan, a beautiful creature not born to be the stepchild of eagles — the North Americans ("Tierra triste" — "Sad Land" [p. 37]). The poem "Encampment," which frames Marqués' vision of the senselessness of war, depicts nocturnal birds pecking at the dead — described as the crumbs of unconfessed illusions. "A Halt in the Task" likens a tear to a plow that widens the furrow in the author's cheek; "The Dream of Shadows" depicts night as an octopus that spreads its ink over the world.

It is difficult to evaluate Marqués as a poet on the basis of his single burst of verse. The twenty-five year old Marqués showed promise and originality, but for reasons that he never clarified, abandoned this literary form.[5] However, the bold imagery of this early poetry recurs in other genres — notably in the short story.

CHAPTER 4

Essays

M ARQUÉS' essays of the fifties, sixties, and seventies reflect his concern with the social and literary trends of his epoch. Eight of the thirteen essays selected for the volume *Ensayos* (1953–1971) characterize Puerto Rico's fundamental social problems. Marqués' prologue specifies his purpose: to clarify some of these enigmatic problems for the next generation. The remaining five essays concern contemporary literature — specifically the Puerto Rican short story and Latin American theater.

I Essays on Society

Marqués' historical essays trace domination of Puerto Rico by the United States and articulate Marqués' critique of this colonial situation — a direct iteration of the concepts that he dramatizes in his plays. Marqués describes how by the midforties, U.S. economic domination had transformed the island's geography ("Literary Pessimism and Political Optimism in Present-day Puerto Rico"). Under U.S. domination, economic emphasis shifted from agriculture to industrialization. Operation Bootstrap, or "Fomento," created in 1942, promoted manufacturing. At first the government owned factories, but by 1947–1948, government plants were sold, and steps were taken to attract industries and capital from the United States. Operation Bootstrap, managed by the Economic Development Administration, offered manufacturers such incentives as exemption from corporate income tax for the first ten to seventeen years of operation. By the 1950s, many more manufacturing plants were established on the island, and as Gordon K. Lewis points out, "By 1957 industry had supplanted agriculture as the major income-earning ingredient of the economy; . . . "[1]

The land was abandoned, as Puerto Ricans emigrated to the city, and eventually to the mainland, in search of employment and material well-being. For many, the "promised land" brought disillusionment, reflected in increasing juvenile delinquency in the cities of Puerto Rico and in the "Puerto Rican problem" in New York City. For Marqués, the worst aspect of this industrialization was its artificiality and its consequent failure to meet the agriculture and commercial needs of the island. He emphasized that in the process, Puerto Rico had become dependent on foreign interests, conveniences, and culture (see "The Docile Puerto Rican," *Ensayos,* p. 193). Marqués points to the 1953 report by Nathan Koenig, subsecretary of federal agriculture, which decried the abandonment of agriculture. In light of this report, Governor Muñoz Marín attempted in 1955 to stimulate agricultural production and marketing; but attempts to develop the valley of Lajas exposed the fundamental defects in the planning and execution of this project (See "Literary Pessimism...," p. 60).

To those who valued "progress" above all, enthusiasts of independence for the island presented a threat to the economic improvement of Puerto Rico. Official political strategy aimed at discouraging independence. During his tenure as governor (1948–1964), Luis Muñoz Marín discredited such terms as independence, nation, liberty, calling them obsolete. He used the rest of Latin America to exemplify the evils wrought by independence. Marqués tells us:

Those who have still not lost their memory in Puerto Rico will be able to remember how many times in the last twenty years [1939–1959] official spokesmen took the "backward" countries of Latin America as a vital example of what the "republic" would bring in terms of hunger, barbarity, disorder, violence, crime, and political setbacks.

(Los que aún no han perdido en Puerto Rico la memoria, podrán recordar cuántas veces en los últimos veinte años los voceros oficiales tomaron a los "atrasados" países de América Latina como ejemplo "vivo" de lo que la "república" traería al pueblo en términos de hambre, barbarie, desórdenes, violencias, crímenes y atrasos políticos ["Literary Pessimism...," p. 74].)

Nationalist outbreaks — attempts against President Truman in Washington (October 30, 1950), against Luis Muñoz Marín in the same year, and against members of Congress in session by nationalist Lolita Lebrón (1954) — were quelled. Albizu Campos, jailed for nationalist outbreaks in the 1930s, was again arrested.[2] The establishment of the Protectorate or Commonwealth in 1952 seemed to be an expedient for solidifying "needed" economic and political ties with the United States (although it was promoted as a "reform" measure to end colonialism).

Marqués stresses the increased contamination of Puerto Rican culture during these years, referring to the increasing emphasis on English in schools, clubs, newspapers, and so forth. In 1960, Marqués pointed out in "Idioma, política y pedagogía" ("Language, Politics and Pedagogy") that the problem of English in education had been resolved twenty years earlier when the Puerto Rican Department of Public Education realized the detrimental effect of teaching academic material in a language that was not the vernacular and adopted as official policy instruction in the Spanish language. Marqués therefore attacks the plan of Cándido Oliveras, secretary of public education in Puerto Rico, to intensify the teaching of English in the public schools. Without denying the commercial and cultural value of learning English, Marqués rejected English as a substitute for the native language.[3]

In "Las tres vertientes del problema del idioma" ("The Three Slopes of the Language Problem"), Marqués laments the fact that in a colonized country such as Puerto Rico, pedagogy is put at the service of politics. "El ruido y la furia de los críticos del Señor Kazin" ("The Noise and Fury of the Critics of Mr. Kazin") sees Marqués attacking an educational system that indoctrinates children with the belief that Puerto Rico cannot stand without the support of the United States and that as children of the colony, they will become authentic, loyal, unconditional North American citizens, because only in that way can they take care of their tender skins and delicate stomachs. He is careful to point out that others, including foreigners, have criticized Puerto Rico's educational system, referring specifically to the American writer and literary critic Alfred Kazin and the sociologist Clarence Senior ("The Three Slopes...," pp. 148–49).[4]

In "Un personaje del folklore y un tema puertorriqueño de farsa" ("A Character from Folklore and a Farcical Puerto Rican Theme"), an essay that serves as a prologue to his drama *Juan Bobo and the Lady of the Occident,* Marqués decries the devaluation of indigenous culture in the university and blames this development on the efforts of former rector Jaime Benítez to "Occidentalize" the University.[5] Marqués states that the tendency to divest the Puerto Rican of his essence and identity has had different names since 1898: North Americanization, universalism (discussed in Marqués' essay "Un autor, un intríngulis y una obra" [An Author, a Plot, and a Work]), and now Occidentalism. In "Literary Pessimism...," Marqués is quick to point out that Jaime Benítez's policy of Occidentalism contradicts Governor Muñoz Marín's policy of "Operación Serenidad" ("Operation Serenity"), established in the fifties for the purpose of promoting the arts and restoring prestige to indigenous Puerto Rican culture.

For Marqués, the history of Puerto Rico has been basically static since the 1930s. Its domination by North America has only been aggravated. Marqués blames not only the colonizing power, but also any submissive Puerto Rican, be he a leader or the man in the street, who seeks at the expense of independence the fulfillment of personal needs.

In his well-known essay "The Docile Puerto Rican," Marqués examines the Puerto Rican's resignation to his dependent condition and his sense of "inferiority" in the face of the North American. Marqués describes the relationship in terms of a colonial guilt complex. In order to tolerate his humiliating condition, the Puerto Rican considers himself inferior to the North American. This unconscious admission of inferiority naturally injures his ego, often provoking extreme compensatory reactions that can take the form of violent antagonism or total surrender.[6]

The violence that pervades Puerto Rican literature might suggest a spirit of resistance rather than of docility. But Marqués insists that violence almost never stems from independence ideology and the urge to end colonialism, but rather from personal frustration, a feeling of weakness and inferiority in the face of the stronger power, and a sense of personal guilt over Puerto Rico's colonial status. Violence is rarely perpetrated against the aggressor. In the short story "El soldado Damián Sánchez" ("The Soldier Damián Sánchez"), by Emilio Díaz Valcárcel, the soldier Damián, victim of the prejudice of his North American companions and officers in Korea, does not unleash his fury against them, but against the Korean friend whom he beats unjustly and viciously. The Korean friend is a step below in the pecking order — the only being whom he can at that moment consider inferior to himself.

Marqués notes that the Puerto Rican nationalist may also direct his frustration and guilt feelings against himself in the act of suicide: "This repressing or inhibiting the normal aggressive impulse toward others, to direct it morbidly against himself"

("Este reprimir o inhibir el normal impulso agresor hacia los demás, para dirigirlo morbosamente hacia sí mismo,..." [p. 161]).[7] For Marqués, the history of nationalism must record not cohesive revolutionary doctrine and action against the invader, but the docile acceptance of North American "superiority," guilt over the colonial state of the country, and the subsequent suicidal impulse. For this reason, it has been a history of failure.[8] In his essay "The Noise and Fury of the Critics of Mr. Kazin," Marqués concurs with Kazin's account of the Puerto Rican as docile. In the face of the criticism leveled against Kazin by North Americans and Puerto Ricans alike, Marqués states that Puerto Ricans need desperately to swallow the dose of truth that Kazin — like Marqués — has given them.

For Marqués, the writer's mission is difficult, since he must fight against the web that others construct to impede his search for truth ("The Function of the Puerto Rican Writer at the Present Moment"). In "Literary Pessimism...," Marqués describes the difference between the politician who is generally optimistic and accepting of the status quo and the writer who is generally pessimistic and critical. He states that pessimistic literature exposes truth and therefore irritates the government[9]: "It is not politically desirable for those in power to have exposed to public light negative or somber aspects of the *status quo,* not even under the winged cloak of Poetry" (" No es políticamente deseable para los responsables del poder el que se expongan a la luz pública los aspectos negativos o sombríos del *statu quo,* ni aun bajo el alado manto de la Poesía" [p. 80]).

Instead of accepting a literature that could fortify the government with constructive criticism of its policy, the government strives to curb the writer. In "Mensaje de un puertorriqueño a los escritores y artistas del Perú" ("Message from a Puerto Rican to the Writers and Artists of Peru") Marqués identifies various forms of censorship that affect the writer: collaboration with newspapers and magazines is impeded; blacklisting prevents publication of particular works or authors; religious proselytizing is used to destroy artistic or literary movements; works and writers are judged from a purely political standpoint. In "Literary Pessimism...," Marqués states that even if critical literature does reach the public, it only serves to relieve their consciences. They can relax, now that "finally *someone* is saying what it was *my* responsibility to say!" ("al fin *alguien* dice lo que era *mi* responsabilidad decir!"

[p. 199]). Marqués claims that the reader then returns to his old way of thinking. He is neither better nor worse for the experience; he remains passive, and no purge or catharsis has taken hold of his character. Despite this pessimism, however, Marqués devotes himself to his vocation as a writer, in the hope that his message will ultimately enlighten his reader.

II *Essays on Literature*

In four essays, Marqués concerns himself with art and literary criticism. "Un autor, un intríngulis y una obra" (An Author, a Plot, and a Work) contains Marqués' analysis of Emilio Belaval's drama *La muerte (Death),* which depicts tourists at a resort in the Balearic Islands who bare their souls, believing that they have eaten poisoned lobster and will soon die. When they discover that the lobster was not poisoned, they resume their shallow lives. Marqués objects to the portrayal of Monica, born in Latin America, but depicted as European in action and thought. Despite Belaval's attempt to point out the artificiality of the lives of these tourists, Marqués sees in Belaval's portrayal of Monica the author's loss of faith in the Latin American identity that could have provided a dramatic contrast to the hypocrisy of the other characters.

In "El cuento puertorriqueño en la promoción del cuarenta" ("The Puerto Rican Short Story in the Forties"), prologue to his *Modern Puerto Rican Short Stories,* Marqués describes the thematic and technical coming of age of the Puerto Rican short story in the 1940s. Although many themes of the Puerto Rican short story are social in nature, Marqués believes that they have achieved a universal quality. He argues that by adapting not only European, but also North American and Latin American models, the Puerto Rican author has assimilated many trends: suggestion by means of the symbol, the interior monologue, the use of flashback. Marqués welcomes the advancement of the short story in an epoch that also produced anthologies and notes the attention given to this genre by Puerto Rican newspapers and by such literary critics as Concha Meléndez.

"Nacionalismo vs. universalismo" ("Nationalism vs. Universalism") depicts Marqués' concern with the integration of Latin American theater. He pinpoints such inherent problems as censorship and the narrowness of local issues. Marqués proposes the international exchange of theater groups, the establishment of a bank of information on national theater in Latin America, and the encouragement of more translation and publication of theatrical works.

In the essay "Luigi Pirandello: el hombre ante su espejo" ("Luigi Pirandello: the Man before his Mirror"), Marqués pays a tribute to this great writer on the first centenary of his birth (1967). Marqués calls him a precursor of the Theater of the Absurd, and discusses his interest in psychology in the context of his family history. Mention is also made of Pirandello's renewal of traditional dramatic devices — including the chorus and the mask. Marqués makes reference in this essay to the work of such dramatists as Beckett, Ionesco, and O'Neill, whose influence on him will become more obvious in a discussion of his drama.

One last essay remains in this collection: "La leyenda hebrea de Abrahán, Sara e Isaac" ("The Hebraic Legend of Abraham, Sarah and Isaac"), which is a justification and explanation of the author's adaptation of biblical events for dramatic purposes in his drama *Sacrifice on Mount Moriah*.

In his essays, Marqués takes care to define his concepts clearly, and he generally identifies the aim of each article at the outset, stating its scope and limitations. He often resorts to caricature and bitter irony to effect his critique; for example, in his critique of the Catholic church's promotion of English, Marqués suggests a picture of Saint Peter opening the doors of heaven to the strains of the Star Spangled Banner ("The Docile Puerto Rican," p. 181). His essays are highly personal and therefore controversial. For example, Juan Angel Silén denounced Marqués' view of the docile Puerto Rican, and in his book *Hacia una visión positiva del puertorriqueño (Toward a Positive View of the Puerto Rican),*[10] he traces Puerto Rican resistance to domination from the colonial epoch. Juan Angel Silén considers economic submission to be a survival mechanism, refusing to believe that it damages the Puerto Rican's identity. Marqués would probably label this view as docile, but would very likely welcome Silén's attempt to give the nation historical models for resistance.

Even while declaring that the writer need not propose solutions, which would in any case be deemed utopian, Marqués prescribes self-analysis for Puerto Rico. Dealing with his own docility and responsive to historical models of resistance, the Puerto Rican should move on to liberty.

CHAPTER 5

Short Stories

MARQUÉS' short stories provide us with an opportunity to
analyze his stylistic development in a single genre; we will analyze here two collections of narratives: *Another Day of Ours* (1955)
and *In a City Called San Juan* (1960).[1]

I Otro día nuestro (Another Day of Ours)

The seven stories collected in his first volume, *Another Day of
Ours,* treat social and existential themes in a manner reminiscent of
his poetry. The themes of nationalism and time are combined in the
first story, from which the collection takes its title). An aging man
(Albizu Campos) is imprisoned for his nationalist creed and must
confront the passing of an era. An age of sacrifice in the name of
resistance has been reduced to memories; only remnants of the
heroic struggle, such as the flag of independence, remain in his
room. The silence of this room contrasts with the din of the
bustling outside world; a noisy garbage truck symbolizes the
destructive force of the times. Extending his arms to his beloved
city, the old man finds that the world he once knew has eluded him.
In its place he finds a maze of "progress": telephone wires, skyscrapers, foreign banks, and factories. Blond tourists portray the
intrusion of North America into his world. The man, like the Tole-
dan sword that hangs in his room, belongs to a past epoch. Time
passes, irrevocably and visibly. Marqués frequently mentions the
changing position of the sun, as another day passes in the man's
dreary life. This Christ figure awaits his ultimate sacrifice: he leaves
his quarters, hoping the guards will kill him. Instead, he is only returned to his room, destined to experience once more the passage of
time, which loses meaning in the vacuum of his room.

Marqués here relies on flashback to fill in his character's past and to explain his motivations. A chance association may stimulate a vision of the past. When the old man's eye falls on some old books, he thinks of one volume inscribed by his friend Juan and then recalls other memories of Juan. The consciousness of time passing intrudes even into memories: Juan, who often visited the man in jail, suddenly stops coming to see him.

This story exemplifies how Marqués focuses on a particular social context to demonstrate a universal condition. The old man could be any man of any land or era who suddenly finds himself displaced in time. This striving toward the universal informs the volume's next story as well.

In "Isla en Manhattan" ("Island in Manhattan"), Marqués presents another individual's sacrifice for the sake of justice. Injustice prevails in the social setting of the story, until justice triumphs in the denouement. A flashback recalls how Juanita, a young girl from Lares, was expelled from the University of Puerto Rico after participating in a strike;[2] how she later lost her job when she joined a strike of radio actors in San Juan; how after emigrating to New York she fails to find work because of her "subversive" activities in Puerto Rico. Juanita finds some relief from her predicament when she meets a blond man on the street — but this interlude too becomes tragic: The man forces himself on her, and she is left on the street in the early hours of the morning, money clenched in her hand. After this episode Juanita finally finds employment — prostitution.

The narration of these events returns frequently to the present, offering an overview of the problems faced by most Puerto Ricans and other minority groups in New York. Marqués reflects the emigrant's cultural shock through the juxtaposition of English and Spanish usage. He depicts widespread, devisive prejudice. A man pushes Juanita, telling her: "Take it easy, spic!" (p. 57). Two children, one Puerto Rican and the other black, squabble: "Godammit! That ball is mine! You spic! Let it go! You dirty Puerto Rican!" (p. 59). We hear through an open window the plight of one Puerto Rican wife who must suffer her husband's drunken bouts. Such injustices accumulate. Juanita comes across a group soliciting signatures for a petition demanding retrial for eight Negroes condemned to death for the attempted rape of a white woman. As in "Another Day of Ours," the present evokes associations with the past: Juanita recalls the loss of her virginity — an irreversible injustice about which no one knew or cared. Juanita identifies with

the oppressed minority, refusing to assimilate into the urban
environment that allows and fosters such injustices. She cannot
marry Nico, who has abandoned the ideals he had embraced when
he participated in the university strike in Puerto Rico. Nico
gradually speaks more English than Spanish and prefers to be
called Nick. He refuses to support the condemned Negroes and
threatens to break off his engagement with Juanita if she signs the
petition. Juanita rejects him, choosing to fight for justice: "And
that piece of paper was for her justice. Justice which was in her
hands for the first time" ("Y aquel pedazo de papel era para ella la
justicia. La justicia que estaba en sus manos por vez primera en su
vida" [p. 71]). Marqués focuses on the petition as it circulates in
the crowd; Juanita follows it with her eyes, adding weight to the
decision she must make. She signs the document and feels suddenly
liberated. Hearing the pharmacy clock strike twelve, Juanita
instinctively makes the sign of the cross: "As if in the metropolis
the Angelus of the church in Lares was ringing" ("Como si en la
metrópoli sonara el Angelus de la iglesia de Lares" [p. 73]). She is
at peace with herself.

Marqués introduces music into the story (a device that he uses
more fully in his drama): when Juanita is expelled from the university, as her own world is collapsing, she hears strains of
"London bridge is falling down;..." (p. 61). After the radio
actors' strike she hears the refrain, "Enjoy yourself; it's later than
you think!" (p. 64), which expresses the spirit that motivates her
flight to New York.

Marqués often treats the same subject matter in more than one
genre. The story "Island in Manhattan" is a part of Marqués'
drama The Oxcart; but here it has some significant changes. In the
play, Juanita is raped in San Juan; she reacts to her family's loss of
her respect for her by becoming a prostitute after the family emigrates to New York. Juanita's brother Luis in the drama recalls the
character of Nick. Both gratify their egos by means of their jobs;
both are insensitive to the plight of minority groups in New York
and reproach Juanita for signing the petition. The symbolic caged
canary in "Island in Manhattan" is a nightingale in The Oxcart.
The symbolism in the drama is tinged with irony. Before the family's emigration to San Juan, Juanita's grandfather tells her that
the nightingale must be free or die of rage. His remark anticipates
the family's entrapment when they move first to the city and later
to the continent, abandoning the land and cutting themselves off

from their roots. It foreshadows Juanita's awareness that they are imprisoned in a land of gray tenements, menial factory jobs, unemployment, and discrimination.

In the collection's next two stories, Marqués treats religious issues. "Pasión y huída de Juan Santos, santero" ("Passion and Flight of Juan Santos, Wooden Saint Carver") deals with the resistance of a single individual, Juan Santos, to the attempt by Protestants to undermine the traditional Catholicism of the Puerto Ricans. Juan Santos defends Catholic tradition by defying the minister's ban on saints' feasts and saints' statues and openly challenges this *jíbaro* turned Protestant clergyman. The minister seeks revenge: Juan Santos' statues are burned, and his tools and materials are stolen. The scene is pathetic: as his dog howls mournfully, Juan attempts to salvage a statue carved by his father, but it crumbles into ashes. Juan carries on, carving wooden statues of saints for people's homes. He is ultimately defeated, however; the minister and townspeople beat Juan viciously, burn his home, and drive him out of the area.

Whereas in the first two stories Marqués constantly shifted between present and past, in "Passion and Flight of Juan Santos, Wooden Saint Carver" he opens the story with the denouement. The minister's imposing figure appears in relief against the chapel door, dramatically illuminated by torches. He leads the march on Juan's house with a single command: "Let's go!" ("¡Vamos!" [p. 41]). The rest of the story is a flashback, recounting the events that led to this finale.

Marqués contrasts the minister's duplicity with Juan's sincerity. He likens the minister to the devil, describing his eyes as green and cold, his smile as false. In the opening scene his figure is enveloped in shadows, illuminated only by the artificial light of the torches. In contrast, Juan is depicted in a more natural, pastoral setting, in the natural light of the stars. Falsity triumphs, and as the mob advances, Juan sees lights that seem to be stars; he does not immediately recognize the torches of destruction.

As in his poetry, Marqués uses striking imagery in his prose. He speaks of his protagonist in terms of natural life processes, referring to corpuscles of tradition and culture in Juan's blood, which resist the invasion of the foreign body (the minister and his ideology) that threatens the health and vitality of the rural organism. As in much of his poetry, the imagery is anatomical, but carries social import. The weak townspeople follow the minister because he represents political power; Marqués characterizes them as a collective Sancho Panza: "And with the common sense of a collective Sancho Panza, they dodged shrewdly any compromising fight against possible windmills" ("Y con sentido realista de Sancho Panza colectivo esquivó ladinamente toda lucha comprometedora contra posibles molinos de viento" [p. 45]). The martyred Juan is finally depicted as a Christ figure; when he is driven from the barrio, he is offered the help and sympathy of women described as "Verónicas." Marqués lapses into melodrama in this story, sharply contrasting good and evil. The characters therefore tend to be cardboard shapes, less developed than the protagonists of "Island in Manhattan." In the final paragraph of "Juan Santos," Marqués suddenly breaks into the bitterly ironic voice of his essays. He resorts to moralizing and characterizes the minister's victory as "territory gained for the Lord where the Gospel and the Truth would now reign forever; a country where the converted peasants would devote their talents to the sensible and useful things which the Lord glorifies in Anglo-Saxon fashion in his minute celestial statistics" ("tierra ganada al Señor donde el Evangelio y la Verdad reinarían ya para siempre; campo donde los jíbaros conversos dedicarían sus habilidades a las cosas sensatas y utilitarias que el Señor glorifica sajonamente en sus minuciosas estadísticas celestiales" [p. 55]).[3]

The next short story in the collection, "El milagrito de San Antonio" ("The Little Miracle of Saint Anthony"), is less pessimistic in tone. Marqués portrays the simple *jíbaro's* successful resistance to changing religious values. A Castillian priest refuses to bless an old woman's statue of Saint Anthony, explaining that wooden statues are not true saints. He recommends that she purchase a plaster statue, which would be acceptable to the church. While likening the fatigue of the overworked priest to the weariness of the old woman who has traveled far to have her statue blessed, Marqués emphasizes the difference in their basic attitudes:

In the eyes of the little old woman from Junquillo it is a loving, merciful, familiar, beautiful image.
In the irritated eyes of Father Luis, the wooden saint is something that his ten years' stay on the island has not yet been able to make him accept as an object of devotion.

(A los ojos de la viejecita de Junquillo es una imagen amorosa, piadosa, familiar, bella.

A los ojos irritados del Padre Luis el santo de palo es algo que sus diez años de estadía en la Isla no han podido aún hacerle aceptar como objeto de devoción [p. 75].)

Marqués underscores the old woman's simplicity. She cannot believe that the wooden statue, which has been in her family for many years and has even been renovated by a local saint carver, has suddenly lost its spiritual value. The plaster statues seem strange to her; they remind her of light-skinned Americans and fail to inspire her with devotion. She even doubts that these figures will understand Spanish. The old woman appeals to Saint Anthony, "What shall I do?" ("¿qué hago...?"]p. 79]). As an aggressive merchant urges her to buy a plaster statue, she abruptly leaves. Enlightened by Saint Anthony, she has resolved to keep the wooden statue and wearily sets out on the long journey home — wearing a triumphant smile.

Marqués endows the old woman with a lyrical voice: "The little old lady's voice is like an indigenous song which speaks of archaic things, of liturgies almost forgotten" ("La voz de la viejecita es como canto autóctono que habla de cosas arcaicas, de liturgias casi olvidadas" [p. 75]). Her voice contrasts with the annoyed intonations of the priest and the hollow sales pitch of the merchant.

"El juramento" ("The Oath") contains elements of farce to expose the hypocrisy of the legal system. Marqués ridicules the efforts made to condemn the nationalist activities of a man who in fact is not a nationalist; he is rather the innocent victim of the official hysteria provoked by the Revolt of 1950, as well as by the McCarthy doctrine of "guilt by association."[4] As in "Juan Santos," Marqués begins at the end, as the verdict is read at the "nationalist's" trial. He is found guilty. Closing his eyes, the convicted man reflects on the stupidity of the entire trial and on the absurdity of the verdict. The remainder of the story is a flashback; Marqués reconstructs the senseless events that culminated in the conviction: The accused is arrested and confined for many months before being assigned a lawyer. Disoriented by solitude and fear, he can hardly remember who he is. When a lawyer finally comes to interview the prisoner, he immediately is convinced of his client's guilt. In all this time, the man has never been told the precise accusation against him, although the lawyer assures him it is all on record. The lawyer suggests bribing the jurors, informing his client that it costs more to buy a majority or unanimous decision. In the courtroom, the man is presumed guilty; the function of the trial is simply to substantiate two allegations: witnesses accuse the defendant of smoking a cigarette on the fourth of July instead of saluting the flag and of uttering an oath. The content of this oath is apparently immaterial. When pressed by lawyers to swear that he had never uttered an oath, the man suddenly remembers an incident from his schooldays — an episode that Marqués included in his novel *The Eve of Manhood:* attacked brutally by the school principal for failing to salute the American flag, the child retaliated with an "anti-American" outburst. The admission of this incident now convicts the man and satisfies those who have attributed to him a guilt by association.

Since the human capacity for reason and logic succumbs to irrational, sadistic impulses, Marqués uses animal imagery to characterize the targets of his satire: the judge is a hungry cat; the public prosecutor has the face of an English dog; the jurors are monkeys; the jury foreman is a crocodile. In this absurd context, communication breaks down; the story recalls the Theater of the Absurd. When the lawyer informs his client that despite his obvious guilt, he has been forced to defend him when other lawyers refused, the young man responds by inquiring as to what brand of aftershave the attorney uses. The trial scene is reminiscent of Camus' *The Stranger:* the defendant takes greater interest in the hum of an electric fan than in the court proceedings. The foreman and another juror are equally bored: "The little girl monkey in the second row began to snore with arpeggio musicality" ("La monita de la segunda fila empezó a roncar con musicalidad de arpegio" [*In a City Called San Juan,* p. 121]).

The docility of the accused earns him only a prison sentence. Marqués tells us in his essay "The Docile Puerto Rican" that in "The Oath," the docile personality of the Puerto Rican is carried to its logical extreme. He is incapable of any actions that may alter the course of his destiny. Marqués' double-edged criticism of the society that victimizes political activists and of the individual who permits this victimization recurs in the drama *A Blue Child for that Shadow.*

In "El miedo" ("Fear"), Marqués explores fear and alienation by instilling these qualities in a single Puerto Rican, who identifies his personal insecurities with those of his dependent island. As the man fears walking into a strange bar, so does his island fear being thrust into a strange world — that of its invaders. Both seem to ask,

"What do these strangers want from me?" (" ¿Qué quieren de mí?" [p. 186]). The story delves into the recesses of the mind; Marqués considered the psychological element of paramount importance in short fiction,[5] particularly in the stories of his second collection.

In "La muerte" ("Death"), a sequel to "Fear," the man's fear becomes more specific. This is not the anxiety of the old man of "Another Day of Ours," who has acted and been defeated. This man's defeat stems from his total inability to act; he sees every act as one step more toward death. This fear is substantiated when the man reacts adversely to rigid, stylized store mannequins — an image of death. The apprehensive man finds no solace in the acts or convictions of those around him — in his girlfriend's commitment to religion or in his boss's to pragmatism. He overcomes his paralysis only when he sees a group of young nationalists who are about to begin a peaceful demonstration in Ponce.[6] Seeing the resolve, confidence, and will expressed by their faces, the man concludes that this act gives life meaning, in spite of death. When the police open fire on the unarmed demonstrators, the man acts; he helps a wounded youth raise the flag of independence, and he himself is killed. Commenting on this story in his essay "The Docile Puerto Rican," Marqués writes that his protagonist does not involve himself in the Ponce massacre with any sense of heroism or politics. He has no nationalist ideology; he accepts death as an existential solution. Through this character, Marqués decries the self-destructive impulse — the deathwish — that overrides ideological considerations.

Thus, Marqués treats the persecution of the nationalist ("Another Day of Ours") and the guilt by association attributed to the nonnationalist ("The Oath"). He depicts the changing religious values in Puerto Rico — the rejection of tradition ("The Little Miracle of Saint Anthony") and the abandonment of Catholicism in favor of Protestantism imported from North America ("Passion and Flight of Juan Santos, Wooden Saint Carver"). He shows how the internalization of North American values is hastened by Puerto Rican emigration to the continent ("Island in Manhattan"). Marqués also explores such themes as time, fear, and death, but generally combines the social element with these themes ("Death" and "Another Day of Ours"). He consistently locates man within his social context and only then attempts to project the social to the universal.

Marqués utilizes in his short stories the same stylistic devices that abound in his novel and poetry: parallelism, contrast, striking imagery, flashback. He believes that the short story lends itself to the use of the symbol as a form of poetic synthesis. In this collection, Marqués sometimes weakens his symbolism by explicitly identifying his own symbols. Not satisfied to offer a vision of rigid, stylized store mannequins in "Death," he explains that they are indeed an image of death. In "Another Day of Ours," the sanitation truck is clearly a symbol of destruction and does not require Marqués' clarification. Marqués' use of symbolism is less heavy handed in "The Oath," in which he exposes the dehumanizing political system by using animal imagery.

The short stories that are most aesthetically gratifying ("Island in Manhattan," "Fear," "The Oath," "Death") avoid black and white contrasts. But Marqués' social messages are most clearly enunciated in the stories that are less subtle ("Juan Santos," "The Little Miracle of Saint Antony"). Marqués' conflict between aesthetic and political values becomes more salient in his drama.

II   En una ciudad llamada San Juan (In a City Called San Juan)

In a City Called San Juan (1960) includes a total of fifteen short stories, three of which are reprinted from *Another Day of Ours* ("Another Day of Ours," "The Oath," and "Fear"). Marqués treats the same basic themes and uses stylistic techniques similar to those of *Another Day of Ours,* but this second volume reflects greater artistic maturity.

In the first story, "Tres hombres junto al río" ("Three Men Near the River"), Marqués portrays the Indians' resistance to the idea of the white man's divinity. Adhering to the Christian belief in Jesus' death and resurrection, three Indians drown a white man; they wait near his body by the river for three days, to see whether or not their victim will be resurrected. When his remains only putrify, the myth is destroyed. One of the Indians equates the destruction of the myth of the white man's superiority with freedom for his land: "My nation will be free. It will be free." ("Será libre mi pueblo. Será libre" [p. 25]).

The opening scene seizes the reader's attention with its drama and mystery. We visualize three silent men staring at a corpse. Suspenseful quiet is violated only by the noises of the forest. The only movement is that of ants crawling into the dead man's ear. This mysterious scenario is then explained by means of flashback. We learn of the contamination of the Indian culture: the incursion of the conqueror; the devaluation of Indian tradition; the imposition of the white man's myths; the white man's contradictions and hypocrisy; and the Indian's increasing resistance to the white man's world: "I don't believe in their power." ("No creo en su poder" [p. 21]). Frequent shifts to the fictional present — the progressive decay of the white man's body — reflect deterioration of the Indian heritage, caused by the white man.

In "Purificación en la Calle del Cristo" ("Purification on Christ Street"), two elderly sisters resist the passage of time, refusing to acknowledge that their once "perfect" world has changed. They were once surrounded by riches, parties, gallant young men; all of this gave way to the vicissitudes of time. They must now confront fading beauty, indigence, the death of people near and dear to them. Hortensia, a third sister, has just died of cancer; the two surviving sisters prepare her body in her coffin. They are pursued by American creditors who wish to reclaim their house and convert it into a luxury hotel.

Marqués places his account of these women in a historical context, dwelling particularly on the coming of the Americans to Puerto Rico in 1898. The sisters have resisted change, and therefore time, by attempting to hold onto remnants of their once beautiful world, symbolized by their jewels. The preservation of the past is linked to the theme of guilt: the sisters claim that they are preserving their beautiful world for Hortensia, to compensate for having destroyed her dream of marriage to a lieutenant. Inés reveals to Hortensia that her sister's intended has had a lover — a woman of low social station — and that he has fathered her child. Hortensia closes the doors of the house, shutting out life. The two guilty sisters also remain locked up and attempt to preserve the "beauty" of the house for Hortensia. Since the house is now threatened by creditors, the living sisters make a suicide pact. They set fire to the house, purifying it and themselves from the further contamination of time.

Flashback supplies the sisters' past. Their break with the temporal world is expressed in the image of an isthmus; the sisters destroy the bridge that links the two worlds when they burn their house. Marqués illuminates the psychological process in this story by introducing free-flowing prose that approaches a stream of consciousness. He uses double indirect discourse — a third person narration that adopts a character's point of view, thoughts, and even language patterns — as in the following account of Emilia's state of mind:

Hortensia! Hortensia in her clear blue dress, when she attended the first reception in the governor's palace (the governor general dancing a Mazurka with her older sister beneath the cold gaze of Papa Burkhart). That's it. Hortensia now in San Juan. The school, past in time. And she, Emilia, observing the dazzling world of the colonial palace on that memorable night, beside the imposing figure of her mother. (Mama Eugenia, with her proud bearing of a queen; her hair dark and thick as the wine of Malaga. . . .)

(¡Hortensia! Hortensia, en su traje de raso azul, cuando asistió a la primera recepción en la Fortaleza (el Gobernador General bailando una mazurca con su hermana mayor bajo la mirada fría de papá Burkhart). Eso es. Hortensia ya en San Juan. El colegio, atrás en el tiempo. Y ella, Emilia, observando el mundo deslumbrante del palacio colonial en esa noche memorable, al lado de la figura imponente de la madre. (Mamá Eugenia, con su soberbio porte de reina; su cabello oscuro y espeso como el vino de Málaga...) [p. 30].)

Marqués adapted "Purification on Christ Street" for the stage, expanding the short story into the drama *Los soles truncos (The Truncated Suns)*. The story does not merely comprise an episode of the drama, as does the story "Island in Manhattan," in *The Oxcart*. In this case, the short story has ample dramatic conflict to fuel an entire drama.

The story "Dos vueltas de llave y un arcángel" ("Two Turns of the Key and a Guardian Angel"), like "Island in Manhattan," concerns prostitution. A young woman, rejected by her family after being seduced by a married man, falls into the hands of a procuress. She is sold to Miguel, who acts as both pimp and lover. Whatever security the woman knows is limited to the confines of her room. One day she recalls the pleasures of the country and attempts to escape. She is found and brought back by Miguel, who slashes her back and pours iodine on the wounds. By the following morning he is once again her "protector," providing the only comfort she knows. That morning is the starting point for the story; the young woman deliriously reconstructs the horrifying events of the previous night: the turn of the key, the sound of footsteps, the image of the razor blade, the hellish pain, the iodine, the threats. Recollection of the near past stimulates more distant memories:

her pleading with Miguel not to play games with his razor stimulates the memory of game playing with the married man who first seduced her. She then recalls her disgrace before the family; her mother asks why she failed to pray to Saint Gabriel for protection. Ironically, she later thanks Saint Gabriel for providing her with the "protection" of the procuress and Miguel.

The narration of this story is filtered through the mind of its protagonist. The young woman associates safety with her room and with Miguel. Outside of this context, the world terrorizes her: through her eyes we see prostitutes whose bracelets jangle to the amplified strains of "Papa loves mambo"; pale men with knives stuck in their shoulders; policemen beating helpless victims with their solid sticks; marines urinating like dogs near lightposts; soldiers engaged in sexual acts with small girls; excrement, strewn garbage, hungry cats; laughing old women with painted eyebrows. We hear the noise of motorcycles and smell the offensive odor of perfumed men who seem like women. While communicating his own vision of urban decadence, Marqués also reveals the mental processes of a victimized, terrorized prostitute: "How would she defend herself from that unexplainable world if he [Miguel] did not exist, nor the room with the dusty floor, nor the key which made the sound of tras-tras?" ("¿Cómo se defendería ella de ese mundo inexplicable si no existiera él, y la habitación de piso polvoriento, y la llave que hacía tras-tras?" [p. 69]). Marqués in this way qualifies the young woman's seemingly irrational dependence on Miguel for security. Her cloistered life takes on religious meaning, which restores a kind of innocence to the sex act; she imagines that Miguel takes on the wings of Saint Gabriel, providing her with liberty and a vision of paradise.

In this story Marqués utilizes many sound effects: the clinking of bracelets, the sound of the bills paid to the prostitute, the "click" of the razor, and the sound of the key turning in the lock. Such theatrical effects recur in the next two stories.

In "La hora del dragón" ("The Dragon's Hour"), Marqués again treats an individual's flight from reality. A middle-aged wealthy woman is troubled by menopause and loneliness (her husband is frequently tied up with business; her son is traveling through Europe). She becomes briefly entangled with a man who, though a stranger and her social inferior, strikes her as exotic: Muratti is an Italian seaman who has visited distant places and who has a dragon tatooed on his chest. Her entrace into an alien world is gradual. At the beginning of the story, the woman stops in a bar, a place she would not ordinarily frequent, because she is suffering from dizziness. She is initially repelled, but soon becomes accustomed to the environment, especially when a young man offers her sugar water to alleviate her dizziness. She notices Muratti sitting at the bar, and finds him handsome. He soon asks how she is feeling, and offers her a ride in his brother's taxi. In the taxi, the drowsy woman recalls her lonely life. We hear fragments of conversation with her husband and son:

Is that you dear? I'm calling to tell you that today I will have lunch in Pleamar. A business matter. Boring, of course. You can go to the Casino, if you like. . . .

(¿Eres tú, nena? Te llamo para decirte que hoy almorzaré en el "Pleamar." Asunto de negocios. Aburrido, claro. Puedes ir al Casino, si quieres. . . [p. 85].)

But mom, I am now a man. I can go alone to Europe. I know how to take care of myself well.

(Pero, mami, ya soy un hombre. Puedo ir solo a Europa. Sé ciudarme bien [p. 84].)

Marqués places the woman in a dreamlike setting to make plausible the woman's shift to Muratti's world. Riding in the taxi, she dreams of her son in Europe and is reminded of her own trip to Europe. She addresses Muratti as if he is the conductor of a train that is pulling into Rome, only to wake up to the familiar sounds of tropical insects. When she leaves the taxi and enters a restaurant, Muratti follows her. They drink and dance, and for her, the dragon tatooed on his chest looms larger and larger. Marqués relates the dragon to Saint John's apocalypse (John 20:2–3) of the release of the chained dragon — a dragon now entices the woman to free herself from the fetters of her life. The scene shifts to a bedroom; the sex act is a momentary rebellion against her boring existence. Unlike the prostitute in "Two Turns of the Key," this woman cannot long remain sheltered from reality. Muratti's ship leaves the next day. Their leavetaking is cold; the woman pays him the fare, as if he were merely a taxi driver. We hear the sound of his car starting up, and the woman retreats into empty loneliness. Marqués leaves to us to wonder what the woman will now do with her life; as the story ends, the woman stifles her sobs and runs to her door — a door that does not shelter her from reality, but rather launches her back to the reality of her lonely life.

Again, the present stimulates memory of the past. The woman's vertigo is attributed to the heat, which immediately initiates a flashback: she recalls reporting hot flashes, symptoms of menopause, to her doctor. Sound effects are also used: the ticking of the man's watch, the clicking of the taxi meter, and so forth. As in "Island in Manhattan," music is incorporated into the story; jukebox renditions of love songs anticipate the bedroom scene: "It is the history of a love as no other which made me understand everything good, everything bad" ("Es la historia de un amor / como no habrá otro igual, / que me hizo comprender / todo el bien, todo el mal..." [p. 80]).

In "En la popa hay un cuerpo reclinado" ("In the Stern, There Lies a Body"), Marqués portrays a man who has been dominated by women all his life. As in his essay "The Docile Puerto Rican," Marqués deplores the fact that since the 1940s, Puerto Rican society has become increasingly matriarchal — a phenomenon that he attributes to American influence. The protagonist of the story has never been able to direct his own life: his mother pushed him into a teaching career, though he wanted to become a writer. His wife channels his energies into supplying her with clothes, television sets, washing machines, cars, a new house — items that put the man deeply in debt. When his wife reluctantly bears him a child, the baby falls sick and dies. The new mother does nothing to help; the man himself takes care of the sick child. The man's only relief from this hellish existence is his visits to a town prostitute — a practice begun in his youth. Ironically, he turns to women even for solace. The protagonist finally poisons his wife, places her body in a boat, rows the boat to a certain point, stands up, and castrates himself — actualizing his emasculation by the women in his life.

Like many of Marqués' stories, the tale begins at the end — as the man rows the boat — and the past and present are revealed through the protagonist's free association of sensations and events. This thought flow eventually reveals that the woman is dead. A single sentence accommodates both the flap of the oars against the water and the memory of the tube in his sick child's throat, which at all costs had to be kept clean. As in Faulkner's *The Sound and the Fury,* recollections appear in italics to signal the shift in time and place. The style reflects the desperate chaos of the man's life.

Marqués uses symbolism in the story (a beautiful clawed bird stands for a woman's destructive elimination of a man), as well as sound effects (the "glu, glu" expresses the sound of oars hitting the water).

The next short story, "El niño en el árbol" ("The Child in the Tree"), is a poem in prose. A young boy named Michelín is disturbed and resentful when his father leaves his mother after a quarrel. Michelín vents his anger and frustration first by killing his mother's pet cat, and second, by defacing the statue of liberty in the town square, which he associates with his mother. The boy associates the tall, powerful quenepo tree outside the house with his father. Unaware of her son's free association, Michelín's mother poisons and removes the tree in order to accommodate more people at cocktail parties. Unable to sustain his rebellion against his mother and her world, Michelín swallows leftover poison and dies on his birthday.

The story is structured as a poem, with four "stanzas" or sections, each a scene involving death: the destruction of the cat, the statue, the tree, and finally Michelín. Each scene begins with a vision of the child in the tree, and a question: "Who killed the cat?" "Who assassinated the statue?" "Who assassinated the tree?" And finally, "Who killed Michelín?" Each division offers the flow of the child's thoughts and memories in response to the initial question.

The same family appears with different names in another short story, "La sala" ("The Living Room"). The father has spent ten years in prison for his activities in behalf of independence. Each character recalls the difficult years of separation: the wife recalls the poverty and prejudice she experienced as the wife of a revolutionary. The child recalls the taunts of schoolmates; the father recalls the agonizingly slow passage of time in prison and the narrowness of his prison cell. Society has divided this family, and Marqués presents their struggle to recover their intimacy. The father attempts to make contact with his son by helping with his homework. Reestablishing communication proves a slow process; long silences are broken only by the creaking of the rocking chair.

Marqués' poetic drama, *A Blue Child for that Shadow,* combines these two short stories. He inserts the father's return from prison ("The Living Room"), but immediately provides conflict over the woman's adultery during her husband's absence ("The Child in the Tree"). The drama then portrays the hardships of all three characters during the separation, taken from "The Living Room."

This portrayal softens the image of the mother, shifting blame onto the society that oppressed the revolutionary and his family.

Another strongly political story, "El delator" ("The Informer"), deals with the revenge taken by a Negro and his friends on a man who, by informing on the Negro's brother, was responsible for his imprisonment. The man has been an informer since childhood; Marqués attributes to him the instinctive treachery of Cain: even after a vicious beating, he smiles and fantasizes about his next opportunity for informing.

The tense, dramatic story uses a cinematic technique. As tension mounts before the beating, the informer sits in a bar, observing the Negro and his friends in a mirror. The Negro tells someone that his brother is in jail, but the remark is clearly intended for the informer to hear. The informer feels the fixation of the Negro's eyes, first on the nape of his neck and then on his own eyes. The music in the bar suddenly stops. The bar's neon sign flashes — its color is blood red. The anxious informer drops and breaks a glass. When he asks for the bill and heads for the door, the tension breaks; he is finally beaten by the group of angry men.

Marqués delves into the informer's masochism, rooted in self-hatred. This is not the first beating he has suffered, nor is it the last. As in the story "Two Turns of the Key," Marqués scrutinizes the inner workings of a twisted, self-destructive mind.

In "La crucifixión de Miss Bunning" ("The Crucifixion of Miss Bunning"), Marqués presents a character who is a remnant from another era. The American Southerner Miss Bunning, on her last night in San Juan, where she has played piano in a nightclub, recalls the events of her bittersweet life. She has known romance and passion, for the young Southerner who fathered her child; but she has also experienced the loss of her son in war and the disappointing decline of her popularity in Chicago nightclubs. She eventually accepts an offer to perform in San Juan, where she is applauded despite her outdated repertoire. As she gives her last performance, the woman is aware of hatred in the eyes of a Negro; in the denouement, this Negro brings her to her room where she plays out the emotional finale of her San Juan existence in bed. Marqués stresses her degradation by comparing her to a ravenous, starved cat in the streets. At the same time, he depicts her as a crucified woman: he describes the cross of the church in the plaza, and then shifts his focus to Miss Bunning, whose arms are outspread in the form of a cross. This image is the culmination of the life of a woman who has been victimized by love and hate, pleasure and vengeance, old age and time. When Marqués writes of "atoms dispersed in the San Juan sky" ("átomos dispersos de Miss Bunning en la noche serena de San Juan" [p. 169]), he expresses the disintegration of a human life.

The story takes place in a noisy, crowded San Juan nightclub where the blare of the jukebox contrasts with Miss Bunning's memories of the elegant past. The present stirs memories of the past: young couples in the nightclub spark a vision of her own youth: "Miss Bunning, Miss Bunning, how beautiful you are!" ("Miss Bunning, Miss Bunning, ¡qué bella es usted! [p. 166]), followed immediately by a cruel reminder of her fading beauty: "Old bitch, forget the piano, and go to an asylum!" ("¡Vieja perra, deja ya ese piano y vete a un asilo!" [p. 166]). Jukebox tunes also reflect the woman's life — her loss of emotional security, the impossibility of finding true love.

In "El cuchillo y la piedra" ("The Knife and the Stone"), Marqués again explores the workings of a twisted mind. His protagonist's internal distortions are reflected by his freakish appearance: his arms are too short for his body. He lives with a girl, Marcela, in a shack, having lost his circus job due to alcoholism. Marqués portrays the man's view of reality, distorted by the influence of alcohol. A hallucination provides a dramatic opening to the story; the protagonist sees monster spiders, worms, lizards; men who suddenly become rats, crabs, serpents, bats. The man is fixated on his physical deformity; he fantasizes monsters devouring parts of his body, except for the stunted arms, which are useless even to monsters. He hopes for a miracle — the growth of his arms. Marcela, in contrast, is developing normally without need of miracle. In one hallucination, a young man demands that Marcela be sacrificed. After verifying that in the Bible, Abraham does attempt to sacrifice his son Isaac, the demented man kills Marcela. He describes himself as the monster and commits suicide. The motive for Marcela's sacrifice is unclear: Does he resent her normality? Does he believe that as his blood becomes mixed with hers, he will become normal? Marqués uses the same biblical reference in his drama *Sacrifice on Mount Moriah,* to examine the notion of sacrifice in both an emotional and political context.

In "La chiringa azul" ("The Blue Kite"), Marqués transports us once again to a child's world, describing the pride the child takes in the kite that he built. Marqués contrasts the child's fantasy — sending messages to the stars — with social reality. The boy lives in such a congested part of town that there is not room enough to fly the kite. When he is turned away from the spacious grounds of "Fort Brook" by the English-speaking guard, the child understands only a few words: "Army, club, golf, guests" (p. 195). But he does understand the most basic fact: "the free land within San Felipe del Morro wasn't truly free, but it was sort of a golf club for officials who, in times of peace, have nothing to do" ("el campo libre encerrado dentro de las murallas sanjuaneras de San Felipe del Morro no era libre en verdad, sino que resultaba ser algo así como un club de 'golf' para los oficiales, que en tiempos de paz no tienen nada útil que hacer" [pp. 195–96]). Marqués couches in this episode his denunciation of American control of Puerto Rican territory. Only in San Cristóbal is the boy finally able to fly his kite. Marqués romanticizes the kite's liberation: the kite is olympic, sure of itself, but sensitive to the hand that guides it; it would dip dangerously, but then fly upward once again, arrogant, majestic, serene against the clear blue sky. Suddenly the kite's freedom is interrupted by the appearance of an enemy: a kite that the imaginative child thinks of as the devil. It is red and flies like an eagle. Its tail seems to the child to be a knife. It cuts the string of the child's kite, and the kite flies away. Frantically chasing his kite, the boy comes across a "No Trespassing" sign and a wire fence. Beyond this he can see the military docks and ships.[7] Sobbing, the boy loses sight of his kite. Thus, Marqués symbolically represents the inhibited freedom of his island.

Resistance to the American invasion of Puerto Rico is the theme of this collection's last story, which bears the book's title: "In a City Called San Juan." The story concerns a Puerto Rican who lives in New York, but vacations annually in Puerto Rico. He has never fully committed himself either to New York or to his native land. He describes himself as the shadow of a man, and it takes the insults of an American sailor to turn him into "a man." Meeting the sailor at a bus stop, the man recognizes him as the one who had tried to cut in on him at a dance hall. The sailor asks him for a match, and when he realizes that he has been recognized, asks "Nervous, spic?" (p. 203). The man moves away from the sailor, but cannot completely ignore him. He hears the sailor approaching him — slow, heavy steps (the heel's "tac," the sole's "sha") — and holds his breath. Marqués communicates the man's increasing nervousness and fear by stressing the repeated sound of the sailor's footsteps on the sand.

The sailor stands on grass near the sign "Federal Property," and urinates on the sidewalk — degrading the Puerto Rican territory. The man begins to be conscious that his city is besieged. He reprimands the sailor, who in turn curses the city and wipes his dirty hands on the man's face. The man snatches the gun he was advised to bring to the dance hall and shoots the sailor. Marqués views this act as a kind of political coming of age: "Standing, between the world of the beach and the world of the street, he was, incurably, a man" ("De pie, entre el mundo de la playa y el mundo de la avenida, era, irremediablemente, un hombre" [p. 207]).

The collection *In a City Called San Juan* achieves clear thematic unity. The majority of stories deal with Puerto Rico's condition under foreign control: the Americanization of Puerto Rico ("Purification on Christ Street," "The Child in the Tree"), the problem of urbanization ("Two Turns of the Key"), the boredom of the materialistic bourgeoisie ("The Dragon's Hour"), the increasingly matriarchal structure of Puerto Rico ("In the Stern, There Lies a Body"), the nationalist movement ("The Living Room"), and the inhibition of liberty ("The Blue Kite"). Political resistance is the theme of the first and last story in the collection: resistance to the early Spanish domination of Puerto Rico in "Three Men Near the River" and resistance to the American invasion in the title story. Marqués uses these two episodes to dispel the myth of the foreigner as god. The sailor in "In a City Called San Juan" is referred to as a "diabolic" god; like the Spanish conqueror, he dies by the hand of a native. Marqués' message is evident in these two stories: he rejects the meaningless sacrifice of Marcela and the self-destruction of the deformed man in "The Knife and the Stone," and he endorses aggression that is turned outward and channeled to achieve positive political goals.

In this collection, while engaged in social conflicts, Marqués' characters also evince universal conflicts. At the beginning of the book, Marqués qutoes from Buddha's Sermon of Fire: he depicts the world aflame with the fire of love, hate, enlightenment, birth, old age, death, pain, lament, anguish, suffering, desperation. These qualities and experiences are then realized in the lives of his characters.

Yet even more important than its thematic unity, perhaps, is the collection's reflection of Marqués' growth as an artist. Symbolism is no longer weakened by explanation: Miss Bunning's crucified pose, the emasculation of the man dominated by females sufficiently convey Marqués' message. Symbolism is even developed enough so that one all-embracing image (the blue kite) can fuel an entire short story. In several short stories, Marqués departs from the traditional narrative and turns to a prose that is free flowing and is developed within the inner recesses of the character's mind.

One striking feature of Marqués' short stories is the inclusion of poetic and dramatic technique. Marqués' poetic vein now becomes so developed that one short story — "The Child in the Tree" — becomes an entire poem in prose. The dramatic technique includes not only dialogue, but sensory elements — music, sound effects, lighting, cinematic technique — devices that are more fully exploited in his drama. It would seem that Marqués prefers to appeal to all of mankind's faculties — intellectual and sensory — so as to effect the author's political and humanistic message.

CHAPTER 6

Early Drama

I   El hombre y sus sueños (Man and his Dreams)

MARQUÉS' early play, *Man and his Dreams* (1946) portrays a man's quest for immortality, which is resolved neither in the flesh nor in religion, but in man's works: "It is not what is given to man which immortalizes him. It is in what man gives that the germ of immortality lies" ("No es lo que dais al Hombre lo que lo inmortaliza. En lo que el Hombre da es donde va el germen de lo inmortal").[1] In the denouement of this one act play, a dying man earns his eternal reward by his works: "The man opens his eyes for the first time and fixes them on the blue ray of light which hurts him ... and his face becomes transfigured with a joyful expression" ("El Hombre abre por vez primera los ojos y los fija en el rayo azul que le hiere, empieza a incorporarse y su rostro se transfigura en expresión de alegría" [p. 46]).

Marqués presents other paths to immortality — through the flesh and religion — in a bad light. The protagonist's son — his own flesh — is corrupt. Envious of his father, he has poisoned him and has committed incest with his stepmother. He also attempts to seduce the nurse who is taking care of his father. Religion is no less corrupt. The priest has lascivious intentions on the nurse: "I am going to pray in the neighboring room. Will you join me?" ("Voy a rezar en la habitación contigua. ¿Me acompañas?" [p. 38]). Religion also implies ignorance and superstition:[2] The religious maid envisions death as serpents biting one's flesh and worms gnawing at one's soul.

Marqués goes one step further and uses color symbolism to express his theme. He writes of three shadows in the denouement — red (flesh), black (religion), and blue (man's works); the blue overshadows the "imposters" of immortality and welcomes the man joyfully into eternity.

Man and his Dreams is a thesis drama that polarizes right and wrong and features one dimensional characters designed to emblemize these qualities. The drama's importance, however, lies in the skeletal elements — themes, characters, stage devices — that Marqués developed in his later work. The play, for example, treats man's egotism. Before the figure of the dying man, elevated on a platform, different characters play out their egotistical parts. A poet, a politician, and a philosopher are self-serving: the dying man, we learn, has been an obstacle in the career of the politician, who therefore does not regret his loss. The poet and the philosopher are gratified, for their own insipid literary productions will no longer have to compete with the work of the dying man. The acquisitive instinct is paramount: In return for a "tip," a servant ushers in the three men to see the dying man, but then complains that the amount is hardly worth the risk of losing his employment; guests come to a party (music and festivity are heard throughout the play) in search of money when they "smell" death. In this value system, people become commodities. The stepmother purchases the nurse's promise of chastity when she fears that the nurse may submit to the stepson's advances; the nurse breaks her promise when the stepson, too, offers her money.

In his later social drama, egotism is an important target of Marqués' critical thrust. Here he associates this character trait with the willingness of his countrymen to maintain economic and political ties with North America. Marqués accuses them of indulging the acquisitive instinct at the expense of their island's freedom.

The poet, the philosopher, and the politician who visit the dying man discuss the three different notions of immortality. The poet speaks of religion as the road to eternity, and the politician believes in immortality through the material — perpetuation through reproduction. The philosopher does not — as we might expect — state explicitly that immortality lies in man's work; he speaks rather of utilizing the past in the present, with a view toward the future. For him, immortality inheres in the evaluation of human existence in history. This triumverate reappears in Marqués' drama *Death Shall Not Enter the Palace* (1956). The politician's puppet gestures and empty words in *Man and his Dreams* are developed dramatically in *Death Shall Not Enter the Palace* in the character of Don José (Luis Muñoz Marín).

Marqués experiments in this play with the lighting and sound effects that are so characteristic of his later drama. He uses red, violet, yellow, and blue lights symbolically. The background hum of conversation and party music intensifies the dying man's isolation. Approaching death is marked by traditional devices — the sounds of a dog howling and a distant tolling bell. When the blue shadow representing immortality has successfully warded off symbols of false immortality, the bell peals triumphantly, and the man ascends to eternity. Once the man has died, the funereal tolling seems to be for the living; the stepmother mourns the end of her ambitions when the son and the nurse go off together. The chaos of human life is expressed by a cacophony of sounds — the stepmother's laugh, the tolling of the bell, the party music, the priest's prayer, the howling dog. This chaos gives way to clarity for the man who enters eternity.

The scenery indicated for the drama is limited to the death bed raised on a platform. Marqués returns to the stark stage in his plays of the seventies; in the interim he made use of more elaborate stage directions.

II   El sol y los Mac Donald
(The Sun and the MacDonalds)

In *The Sun and the MacDonalds* (1947), Marqués portrays an established family in the southern United States, a lineage that has remained static for over a century. Attempting to preserve the purity of their blood, the family has resorted to inbreeding.

The clan's narrow existence is threatened when a young son, Ramiro, attempts to escape its confines. Marqués portrays the family's history of isolationism in Act II: A flashback describes incestuous relationships (father-daughter, mother-son, brother-sister, cousin-cousin) in several generations of the family, beginning at the turn of the nineteenth century. The present witnesses Gustavo's incestuous desire for his sister Teodora; Teodora's son Ramiro has a similar feeling for his mother. This inbred family has always vigorously discouraged outsiders from marrying into it; for example, a young woman's French suitor is actually shot by her father. In the present generation, a brother, Gustavo, forbids his sister Elisa to marry her first love when a Negro strain is discovered in his ancestry. Gustavo also suspects another boyfriend, Antonio, of having Jewish blood. The family is plagued not only by bigotry, but

also by jealousies.
Egotism and isolationism have dominated this bloodline for over a century. Gustavo aptly summarizes the family's existence: "But time does not count for the MacDonalds. We are the same. Identical, immutable..." ("Pero el tiempo no cuenta para los Mac Donald. Somos los mismos. Idénticos, inmutables..." [III, 135]). Even when a MacDonald travels, he remains isolated, seeing nothing: "Landscapes that do not reach my heart.... Mountains and valleys.... The tropical sun, and I, in the shadows.... Travel.... How useless,..." declares Gustavo ("Paisajes que no llegan a mi corazón... Montañas y valles... Sol del trópico, y yo, en la penumbra... Viajar... Cuán inútil..." [I, 56]). His life is no less tedious than that of his sister Teodora, who stays in the house and endlessly knits. When Ramiro invites Gustavo to watch boat races at the university, he suggests that seeing his friends in their own environment will be a new experience for his uncle. Gustavo promptly refuses the invitation.

The play does suggest awakenings to the need for a changed life: Gustavo knows that he must examine his own circumstances. Yet he retreats from self-analysis: "Each time that I try to analyze myself I retreat frightened.... I do not want to know how I am. Yes, it is better to not know..." ("Cada vez que trato de analizarme he de retroceder asustado... No quiero saber cómo soy. Sí, es mejor no saber..." [I, 80]). There are those who do reject the darkness of ignorance; the outsider Antonio says that shadows merely protect: "Give me light, much light. Without light I cannot conceive of life. That's why I stay with Elisa. Of course I can't explain how so much light can exist in the midst of so many shadows.... You [the family] love obscurity;... Not Elisa. Elisa loves light, unlimited horizons, laughter, joy..." ("A mí dame luz, mucha luz. Sin luz no concibo la vida. Por eso me quedo con Elisa. Claro que no me explico cómo puede existir tanta luz en medio de tantas sombras.... os gusta la oscuridad;... Elisa no. Elisa ama la luz, los horizontes ilimitados, la risa, la alegría..." [I, 62]). Elisa later switches on the light in the house: "With light to see each other's faces. I cannot get used to the shadows!" ("Con luz para vernos las caras. ¡Ay, no me acabo de acostumbrar a las sombras!" [II, 96]). Despite her efforts, she cannot overcome the family's wish to live in shadows.

Ramiro, on the other hand, attempts to escape this victimization. Liberated by his consciousness of the family's sins, he leaves, declaring ironically that he is not worthy of the family name: "To be a MacDonald and to be dead is the same thing. The alternative is to escape to life" ("Ser un Mac Donald y estar muerto es una misma cosa. La alternativa es escapar hacia la vida" [III, 157]). But the defiant act is not decisive, and Gustavo warns at the end: "The tragedy does not have a final scene..." ("La tragedia no tiene escena final..." [III, 165]), claiming that Ramiro is as oriented toward death as the rest of the family. The statement is ambiguous, but there is a suggestion that Ramiro's incestuous desires will consume him.

As can be seen, Marqués overstates his convictions in this drama, often burdening his characters with wordy monologues. The play also suffers from overworked stage devices (for example, Enrique's suggestion in Act III that he and Teodora see the play *Oedipus*). Its imagery is rather unsubtle: Marqués characterizes the MacDonalds as a family existing within a shell — closed off from foreign influence but rotting from within. It is also associated with obscure shadows, dried roots, a dead tree trunk. As the flashback reveals the clan's decadent history, wind stirs the dry leaves. The image carries over into Act III, where the mention of bare trees suggests the sterility of the family's existence.

Yet *The Sun and the MacDonalds,* like *Man and his Dreams,* contains thematic and stylistic devices that are developed in Marqués' later work. *Sacrifice on Mount Moriah* (1969) also deals with a son's break with corrupt family — the biblical figure Isaac leaves his father Abraham and mother Sarah, seeking liberty from his egotistical, materialistic kin. The same complexity characterizes the later drama: it remains unclear whether or not the son can escape his birthright.

The theme of isolationism is placed in a political context in Marqués' social drama. He shows how Puerto Ricans, caught in the trap of national dependency, fail to perceive alternative solutions for the island's socioeconomic problems. Like Gustavo and other members of the MacDonald family, his countrymen fail to step out of the darkness imposed by a limited perspective. Ramiro, on the other hand, approaches Marqués' ideal. He understands that his world is narrow and is willing to entertain change. By instilling doubt as to Ramiro's success, however, Marqués places himself among those writers who discredit the very solutions they propose.

In this drama, Marqués utilizes the image of the mask. Gustavo speaks often of the family's masked lives. Ramiro, addressing the audience from his more liberated stance, goes one step further, insisting that the mask must slip: "The mask which hides us has to fall today or tomorrow.... Reality does not admit shadows.... The truth cannot be hidden" ("La máscara que nos oculta ha de caer hoy o mañana.... La realidad no admite la penumbra.... La verdad no puede ocultarse" [III, 136]). Marqués later uses actual masks, as did O'Neill in *The Great God Brown* (1925), in his dramas *Juan Bobo and the Lady of the Occident* and *Carnival Outside, Carnival Inside.*

Cinematic techniques are also used in this play; flashback expresses the flow of time. It is dramatized behind a gauze curtain, which Marqués later employed in *Juan Bobo.* The play also contains simultaneous action (a device also used in *Tito y Berenice (Titus and Bernice)* [1970]): a love scene between Elisa and Antonio takes place on the balcony at the same time that Teodora and her husband Enrique are quarreling in the living room.

The Sun and the MacDonalds indicates Marqués' expertise at adapting an influence to suit his own purposes. The title of the play, *The Sun and the MacDonalds,* alludes to a myth in which the sun kills his father (night) and marries his mother (dawn). Teodora's husband explains this myth to his wife in Act III. The myth gave rise to the Greek tragedy *Oedipus,* which was a source for Eugene O'Neill's *Mourning Becomes Electra* (1931). Marqués was very probably influenced by the O'Neill play. However, the sun in Marqués' work has other meanings as well. It symbolizes time — the daily rising and setting of the sun witnesses the unaltered existence of the MacDonalds over many years. Gustavo makes this concept explicit at the beginning of Act III: "The same sun hurts our faces.... The same moon chills our hair with its silver. The same life shatters our hearts.... Everything severe, fatal..." ("El mismo sol hiere nuestros rostros.... La misma luna enfría con su plata nuestros cabellos. La misma vida destroza nuestros corazones.... Todo inexorable, fatal..." [III, 135–36]). The sun also symbolizes moral illumination. Marqués manipulates light and darkness in the play, as we have seen, to suggest various states of moral consciousness. His adaptation of traditional devices to suit his own intents will be seen again in a later drama, for example *The Apartment* (1964).

Marqués' two early plays are embryonic, containing the thematic and stylistic seeds that germinate in later drama, cultivated as they

are by Marqués' growing artistic maturity. These works also indicate a tendency in Marqués' production that remains even in his
mature period: the fluctuation between dramas of thesis (*Man and
his Dreams*) and plays of more complexity (*The Sun and the
MacDonalds*).

CHAPTER 7

Social Drama

MARQUÉS wrote six dramas that deal exclusively with Puerto Rico's social problems. Using diverse dramatic styles — realistic drama, poetic drama, tragedy, Theater of the Absurd, pantomime — Marqués treats such salient issues as economic dependency on North America, industrialization of an essentially agricultural country, emigration, and oppression of the nationalist. In his writings, Marqués clearly espouses the struggle for independence and cultural affirmation. We shall follow the development of his thought, and at the same time, we shall analyze the impact of his dramatic techniques.

I   La carreta (The Oxcart)

In *The Oxcart* (1951), Marqués dramatizes the plight of the *jíbaro* who migrates from the mountains to San Juan and then to New York. The peasant's dreams of improving his economic lot are shattered, undermined by severe family problems that stem from a conflict between his native rural culture and urban life.

Marqués attributes the genesis of the drama to his experiences with the *jíbaro* in the mountains, as well as to his own observations of life in San Juan and in New York:

> In 1951, while a group of filmmakers and I were making the picture "A Voice in the Mountain" in the mountains of Puerto Rico, I met the principal characters of "The Oxcart." I lived with them for three months. It was not, of course, my first intimate contact with the Puerto Rican peasant. As a grandson of farmers — and myself an agronomist besides — the land and its inhabitants had always been an intimate experience of my life.
>
> On the other hand, four years of residence in the capital had permitted me to observe the agony of the peasant adapting himself to the conditions of the San Juan slums. And my studies at Columbia University gave me the opportunity to capture the tragic conflict of that same Puerto Rican

when, tireless in his pathetic quest for an easier material life, he emigrates
to the New York metropolis.

I had, then, at first hand, the material which would constitute the three
dramatic stages of the emigrant family: the Puerto Rican countryside, the
San Juan slums, and the North American metropolis.

(Mientras un grupo de cineastas filmábamos en 1951 y en las montañas
de Puerto Rico la película "Una Voz en la Montaña", conocí a los princi-
pales personajes de "La Carreta". Con ellos conviví durante tres meses.
No era, desde luego, mi primer contacto íntimo con el campesino puertorriqueño. Como nieto de agricultores — y agrónomo además — la tierra y
su habitante habían sido siempre experiencia entrañable de mi vida.

Por otro lado, cuatro años de estancia en la capital me habían permitido
observar la agonía del campesino adaptándose a las condiciones del arra-
bal sanjuanero. Y mis estudios en la Universidad de Columbia me dieron
la oportunidad de captar el trágico conflicto de ese mismo puertorriqueño
cuando, incansable en su patética peregrinación por una vida material más
desahogada, emigraba a la metrópoli neoyorquina.

Tenía, pues, de primera mano, el material que habrían de constituir las
tres etapas dramáticas de la familia emigrante: el campo boricua, el arra-
bal sanjuanero y la metrópoli norteamericana.)[1]

The reasons for the family's migration are social and historical.
One time landowners and coffee growers, the family was reduced
to poverty by the decline of interest in coffee cultivation, and by the
imposition of the sugar cane monoculture. The inability of Doña
Gabriela's late husband to adjust to the changing economy had
accelerated the family's economic downfall. Doña Gabriela tells us:
"he never understood sugar cane. He didn't like it. He always
dreamed about coffee."[2] Gordon K. Lewis adds that by 1940 even
the sugar monoculture could no longer cope with the fact that "the
competition of mechanized beet and cane sugar both in the con-
tinental states and in the duty-free offshore areas (Hawaii and the
Phillipine Islands), combined with relative high production costs as
compared say with the Cuban industry, had caused the Puerto
Rican industry to come to a relative standstill." The tobacco industry was also in decline and "the traditional high-class Puerto Rican
coffee..., never recovered from the loss of its world markets during
the First World War,..." Lewis notes a "hazardous dependency
upon agricultural production" resulting in "a burgeoning neo-
industrial society."[3]

This economic transition generates Marqués' central dramatic
conflict in *The Oxcart*. When the family cannot pay the mortgage

on their land, one of two options is possible: migration to the city to seek economic betterment or peón existence in the country. Marqués translates this into the conflict between Doña Gabriela's father, Don Chago, who focuses on love for the land and her adopted son Luis, who resents the *peón's* role and opts for urban industrial existence. Don Chago's determination to work the land, despite poverty, is being rebuffed by Luis, who represents a new generation seduced by the promise of economic gain.

Since Luis is the accepted head of the family, the other family members — Doña Gabriela and her children Juanita and Chaguito — support his decisions. Yet Marqués emphasizes that all three are still attached to the land. Doña Gabriela becomes nostalgic when she thinks of her childhood days in the country, her courtship with her husband, and the birth of their children. And she concentrates on bringing remnants of the land with her, such as "the little clump of mint" (I, 41), and keepsakes of her religious, spiritual life, such as the wooden statue of Saint Anthony. Juanita has a romantic interest in staying in the country — her attraction to the *peón* Miguel. But she does not resist the move. The culturally enforced docility of the Puerto Rican woman prevents Juanita from expressing her true feelings, except in the presence of her grandfather. Chaguito struggles between his attraction to economic advancement and his attachment to the land. On the one hand, he looks forward to earning money in the city; on the other, he pathetically hides his rooster, which Doña Gabriela and Luis wish to sell to Miguel.

The dramatic conflict between the old and the new, the secure and the unknown, is heightened by the family's fond memories of their past life on the land. In a highly dramatic scene, Marqués describes their feeling of indecision when they hear the oxcart approach: "There is a moment of immobility among the characters. A great shadow of anguish passes over them, a mute interrogation of the future, a fear of tomorrow, a desire not to act, to remain fixed and allow the fascination of the cart to pass by" (I, 44). But almost simultaneously, Luis breaks the spell and initiates the move.[4]

In Act I, Marqués' position against emigration is artistically couched in references to the cage in which Juanita wants to place a nightingale, in Don Chago's description of Luis' seriousness as something that makes him "as sorrowful as the dead" (I, 19), and in Luis' comment that night is coming. Marqués believes the family is doomed to imprisonment, death, darkness, because they are leaving the land, their roots, their source of identity.

In the rest of the drama, Marqués catapults the family toward doom by means of a rather overworked melodrama. In San Juan, the family experiences a bitter struggle with poverty, filth, noise, child abuse, prostitution, and so forth. Juanita is raped, undergoes an abortion, and attempts suicide. Luis is seduced by Doña Isa, wife of the café owner Don Severo, who wishes to alleviate her husband's conscience (Don Severo has been carrying on an adulterous affair with Luis' girlfriend Martita). Chaguito is absorbed by the city and the delinquency it fosters. He is arrested for stealing and placed in a reform school. In New York, family alienation is most severe: Juanita no longer lives at home and has turned to prostitution (Luis' closer watch over Juanita after the San Juan misfortunes is instrumental in her decision to move). Luis is completely assimilated into the industrialized world. He becomes insensitive to everything surrounding him (including Doña Gabriela's homesickness), overwhelmed as he is by love for the machine and the factory. Yet the machine causes his death: As he examines the interior of one of the machines, Luis is killed when it suddenly begins to operate.

Irony is also overworked in the drama. In Act II, Luis' dreams of economic improvement have been shattered. After working at five jobs in a single year, Luis is unemployed. Ultimately, the only position Luis can secure in the city is that of a gardener; he cultivates the land. Doña Gabriela, in her delight, muses upon this ironic salvation: "You know somethin', Luis? You came to the city to get away from the land. And now the land helps you out right here in the city" (II, 79).

The family's dishonor is also ironic. In Act I, Marqués establishes Doña Gabriela's profound sense of honor, her objection to Juanita's interest in Miguel, and her belief that emigration will save the family's honor. She tells Luis in Act I that nothing has happened between Juanita and Miguel to shame the family, "But if we weren't gettin' out o' here now, somethin' could've happened" (I, 22). In Act II, dishonor befalls not only Juanita, but also Luis and Chaguito.[5] And the irony is intensified by the decision to emigrate once more, this time to New York, where Juanita's prostitution will increase, rather than dispel, family dishonor.

The machines that provided economic sustenance for Luis ironically bring his death. And his body is, again ironically, transported back to Puerto Rico — the land that he abandoned in life and that will now accept him in death. Implicit in this irony is Luis' personal dilemma. He is searching for a mother figure, but at the same time alienates himself from his "mother" Doña Gabriela and his motherland.

Luis' character is one dimensional and relatively undeveloped, for he must serve Marqués' thesis. He represents the destiny of many Puerto Rican youths who dream of settling in a material paradise in an industrial world. They alienate themselves from their roots, like Luis, saying: "Of course, it'd be easier up there. They say there's plenty o'work. They pay good. An' the poor man's as good as the rich" (II, 81). Luis is manipulated by a destiny over which he seems to have no control. The prospect of future migration to New York dominates his thoughts even while he is still in the mountains. He describes the ships that he will be able to see from his house in San Juan as "ships that take you to other lands. And airplanes too. Big birds that come and go. That'd be good, wouldn't it. To go far away, real far. . . . To New York, maybe. . ." (I, 25). The tension between two worlds is always present, as in the scene in which Juanita views the model oxcart; bucolic music is drowned out by the noise of an airplane overhead. For Luis, the appeal of the land is overpowered by the dream of migration and urbanization.

Notwithstanding his one dimensional character, Marqués does invest Luis with the role of a tragic hero — a man whose limited vision causes his fall.[6] Yet the tragic element is obscured, for Marqués' insistent political orientation makes his vision of life in *The Oxcart* more melodramatic than tragic.

Doña Gabriela's character is somewhat more highly developed. Her strong character, undermined in the city, is fortified by a letter from her brother Tomás, who offers the family land to cultivate if they wish to return to Puerto Rico. Yet her realization of the family's alienation and her desire to return to the land cannot find expression as long as Luis is alive. She is bound by her role as mother and protects the insecure Luis who is head of the family. She supports his decisions, stifling her true feelings. In a sense, her ties to the culture precipitate the tragedy. Her desire to return to the land can only materialize after Luis' death.

Juanita experiences the most growth. New York has a pervasive influence on her character. She challenges Luis' concept of honor — the double standard that obligates the woman, but not the man, to maintain honor. She defies this concept by becoming a prostitute. Juanita sympathizes with the typically enslaved Puerto Rican woman. Her reaction against the Puerto Rican woman's inferior status, both in Puerto Rico and in New York, is reinforced by her neighbor Lidia who suffers with an unemployed husband and a sick child, but prefers her situation to the physical and emotional isolation of life without a husband.

Juanita's concern about inequality extends beyond the feminist issue; she has also begun to discern the oppression of minority groups in New York, the oppression of all emigrants. She becomes indignant at the death of several Puerto Ricans in a Harlem fire, blaming the landlord who did not provide a fire escape. She is outraged when the police kill an unarmed Negro Puerto Rican boy who was trying to rob an American woman's wallet. Juanita is puzzled and outraged by judicial inequalities when she learns of the sentencing of seven Negroes for attempted rape of a white woman. She reflects on the imbalance between this extreme sanction against those who attempted rape and the total lack of punishment of the man who actually abused her. She also thinks of the emotional punishment she has suffered at the hands of her family. Juanita recognizes that the minister's rejection of the Puerto Ricans' "inferior" Papist-Catholic beliefs stems from his desire to impose his own religion on the Puerto Ricans. Conversion, he promises, will make them good Americans, and free them from discrimination.

These events in Act III have been criticized for their "episodic" character.[7] Yet, although excessive, these incidents communicate the "realistic" oppression of the Puerto Rican in New York, at the same time that they give Juanita the experience necessary to develop her awareness and to prepare her for her return to Puerto Rico after Luis' death. Because of these experiences, Juanita eventually concludes that survival for the individual Puerto Rican depends on a sense of community with others who share his roots. And this involves a return to the land.

Marqués' dramatization of the misunderstanding of the experience and needs of Puerto Ricans and other minority groups in Act III also serves another function: the episodes parallel family misunderstanding, especially Luis' lack of comprehension of the needs of Doña Gabriela and Juanita.

The use of "realistic," regional language (the aspiration of the final "s," the use of "l" instead of "r") in *The Oxcart* has also been criticized.[8] But Marqués, writing more for an audience than for the reader, wishes to represent the family's real situation, including speech patterns. A more standardized Spanish would have impoverished the *jíbaro's* cultural setting. The frequent use of English words made hispanic in Act III — *marqueta, grocería, lonchera* — mark the *jíbaro's* increasing assimilation into the New York environment.

Notwithstanding the play's overworked irony, its melodrama that obscures the tragic element, its "excessive" episodes and "realistic" language, *The Oxcart* does contain many highly dramatic moments (the already mentioned arrival of the oxcart in Act I; Doña Gabriela's discovery of Juanita's abortion in Act II) that are carefully detailed by Marqués in stage directions. He describes the scene of the abortion in the following way: "As Luis is about to arrive at the bedroom, Da. Gabriela appears in it. Her arms hang inertly beside her body. In one hand she holds the bottle of alcohol. Luis remains still. Their eyes meet. The bottle of alcohol falls to the floor. There is a terrible silence broken only by the beating of the waves on the rocks" (II, 100).

What is also striking about the play is Marqués' portrayal of the family's tragic alienation not only with action and dialogue, but also with visual and sound effects. We have already seen in Act I that tradition is represented by such concrete objects as the rooster and the statue of Saint Anthony. But in the second act, these props disappear (both Chaguito's rooster and Doña Gabriela's spiritual treasure are sold). Those symbols of tradition that do not disappear altogether, for example the old rocking chair, are placed in an ugly, dirty setting. The grandfather's traditional song — the spicy folkloric "plena" sung in Act I — gives way to the deafening blast of a jukebox in Act II. Bucolic music and the familiar voice of an oxcart driver are drowned out by the roar of the airplane. The only music in Act III is the American "blues." This act is dominated by the roar of the subway and the noise of the automatic drill used by workmen repairing the street. Tradition survives only in the model oxcart that Miguel sends to Juanita. Symbolizing the land, it also symbolizes migration; and it anticipates the family's migration back to the land in the denouement.

II   Juan Bobo y la Dama de Occidente
(Juan Bobo and the Lady of the Occident)

Visual and auditory elements alone comprise Marqués' next

drama, *Juan Bobo and the Lady of the Occident* (1955), where Marqués expresses his social message in a new genre — pantomime. Marqués mirrors his country's rejection of its own culture and its pursuit of "Occidental" values (represented in the figure "The Lady of the Occident"). Puerto Rico is far from oriental; yet Marqués employs the term "Occidental" to characterize those North American and European values that Puerto Ricans have adopted while denying their own essence. One of the chief promoters of this tendency is former rector of the University of Puerto Rico, Jaime Benítez, whose plans to "Occidentalize" the University of Puerto Rico are criticized by Marqués. This play functions as a kind of wish fulfillment for Marqués, for he dramatizes resistance to "Occidental" values, investing the folklore character Juan Bobo[9] with fidelity to his first love — Puerto Rico. At the same time Marqués fantasizes North American acceptance of, and respect for, Puerto Rican culture.

The *jíbaro* Juan is at first unconscious of his need to identify with Puerto Rico and seeks affiliation with an alien culture. His resistance to certain aspects of this culture eventually surfaces, and he finds the strength he needs to develop as an "ideal" Puerto Rican.

The drama's message, conveyed without the spoken word, requires precise visual and auditory effects. The villain professor (who is not unlike Jaime Benítez) is a grotesque creature, puppet-like in appearance and gesture, whose nervous movements recall St. Vitus' dance. He makes villainous gestures when he deceives Juan. His speech, in pantomime, on the merits of the Lady of the Occident, is mechanical: its artificiality reflects the culture that the professor is attempting to impose on his nation. His prop is also visually symbolic: the diploma needed to enter the Occidental world is large (Puerto Rico's conception of the bigger, the better) but unwieldy (for it is a false culture for Puerto Rico).

Juan's pursuit of the Lady of the Occident is also portrayed visually. In Scene III, in the tower of the University of Puerto Rico, Juan faces a series of platforms to the right and the left, leading up to the figure of the lady, who stands on the highest estrade. On lower platforms, posters representing Western literary works appear; Juan interacts with characters from these works who step out from behind the signs. The lady is the "superior" value that can only be attained by passing through the cultural landscape of the Occident. These Occidental cultural qualities include Electra's bloody vengeance; Machiavelli's political treachery; prostitution as seen in *La Celestina;* the compromise of conscience as seen in Goethe's *Faust;* Lady Macbeth's fatal ambition; Jean-Paul Sartre's intellectual nausea. Arthur Miller's salesman urges Juan to buy something he does not need; Tennessee William's Blanche Dubois makes advances toward him.

We cannot mistake what these characters represent, for Electra's tunic and hands drip blood; Machiavelli's treachery is emblemized by a sword and a vial of poison; Celestina displays her amulets for winning over a loved one; Mefistófeles buys souls with a check from National City Bank; Lady Macbeth, like the prince, carries a sword; the salesman Willy Loman peddles his wares — an ice bag and vegetable brush.

Marqués utilizes the mask in this drama, giving it a double purpose. It provides mystery and attraction in the case of the lady at the outset, covered as she is by a large blue veil. In the denouement, however, the lady's mask is cold, inexpressive, dead — symbolic of the Occident's insensitivity to Puerto Rico. Yet this deadness ends when the mask is removed. Now cognizant of Juan's need to affiliate himself with Puerto Rico, and not with the Occident, the lady proceeds to place the character at his sweetheart's (Puerto Rico's) side.

Some of Puerto Rico's other problems are portrayed in this drama, again by visual devices. In Scene II, Juan puruses the "señorita" of upper class Spanish society, convinced as he is that she is his mysterious lady. When he tries to approach her, he is inhibited by the social barriers that separate the Spanish and indigenous Puerto Ricans, stemming from Spain's history of imperialism on the island. Effectively utilizing a gauze curtain to pinpoint this serious division, Marqués tells us of the señorita and Juan Bobo:

they are two social spheres which do not touch. Juan dances in the foreground, in silhouette, while she dances in the background under the white and blue light. From time to time her figure, illuminated, and his figure, in silhouette, approach the gauze and they dance several steps in unison, but she flees again to her inaccessible world.

(son dos esferas sociales que no se tocan. Juan baila en primer término, en silueta, mientras ella baila al fondo bajo la luz blanca y azul. De vez en cuando la figura de ella, iluminada, y la de él, en silueta, se acercan a la gasa y dan algunos pasos al unísono, pero ella vuelve a huir a su mundo inaccesible.)[10]

Sound effects are also expertly utilized. When Juan runs to the cultural landscape of the Occident, there is musical cacophony, suggesting the cultural confusion faced by the Puerto Rican who submits to the alien culture. When Juan passes through the maze of the Occidental landscape, he ingeniously dodges each threat by perceiving its danger. Juan's victory in each instance is emphasized by thunder and lightening and the fall of the literary character.

Music contrasts the two cultures: Indigenous music — the *plena, seis, bomba, danza puertorriqueña* — clashes with the American blues and the jitterbug. In contrast to *The Oxcart,* where the folkloric *plena* gives way to the blare of the jukebox, symbolic of the family's alienation from its tradition, in *Juan Bobo,* the reverse takes place. A jitterbug captivates Juan in his immature period; yet later on, when Juan rejects Mefistófeles' offer of material gain in exchange for his conscience, we hear the melody of the *plena* "Santa María."

By means of music, Marqués depicts another serious Puerto Rican problem: racial intolerance. At the beginning of the drama, Juan is engaged to the "Novia" or sweetheart who represents Puerto Rico. During the festivities that mark this event, the timid Juan shies away from his own group of *jíbaros,* preferring not to join a group dance. But he soon learns to celebrate his own cultural roots and dances joyously with the mountain *jíbaros.* The *jíbaro* dance of the *seis* is interrupted by the music of a group of Puerto Rican Negroes and mulattoes from the coast, who dance the *plena.* At first the two groups remain separate, but before long a mulatto woman begins dancing with a white *jíbaro;* a Negro man dances with a peasant girl, and a mulatto offers a drink to Juan Bobo. The two groups merge and happily dance the *plena.* This spirit of tolerance among the various racial groups that form the basis of the Puerto Rican population is not usual in North America. Nor is it typical in Puerto Rico: Maxine Gordon, in "Cultural Aspects of Puerto Rico's Race Problem," points out: "the designated position of inferiority which the Puerto Rican Negro or Mulatto often occupies in his own opinion as well as that of others."[11] Marqués decries Puerto Rican racial intolerance, viewing racism as an imported North American attitude, especially in relation to the Negro. By means of dance and music, he offers his vision of racial confraternity as a form of resistance.

This play reflects Marqués' increasingly sophisticated dramatic technique, yet it was not well received in Puerto Rico. The drama was censored on the basis of its critical social stance. The Ballet

Corps of San Juan did not produce the drama that it had com-missioned.[12] The satirical attack on Jaime Benítez caused the ballet's directors, who receive subsidies from the government and the university, to reject the play as inappropriate. They chose to produce instead *Juan Bobo y las fiestas (Juan Bobo and the Cele-brations)* in the Seventh Festival of Puerto Rican Theater in 1959 — a play with a more superficial and festive content.

This censors' action seems to substantiate Marqués' own view that critical literature threatens the government more than society. He laments the government's rejection of *Juan Bobo*, which he believes could have given the nation "a clearer perception of adverse realities" ("una más clara percepción de realidades adver-sas") and which could have "fortified the very government of which it is, directly or indirectly, a live reproach" ("robustecer al mismo gobierno del cual es, directa o indirectamente, vivo reproche").[13]

Despite censorship, Marqués has carried on with his social mis-sion as a writer. His penchant for couching his social message in a variety of theatrical forms is continued in the next drama, *Death Shall Not Enter the Palace*. Here Marqués portrays what he viewed as the tragedy of the year 1952: Governor Luis Muñoz Marín signed and agreed to the Commonwealth with the United States, dealing a serious blow to the island's aspirations for liberty.

III   La muerte no entrará en palacio
(Death Shall not Enter the Palace)

In *Death Shall Not Enter the Palace* (1956), Marqués presents elements of tragedy at the very apex of Puerto Rican society — in the governor's palace. He dramatizes how one man's limited vision can cause his ruin and the ruin of his nation. Governor Don José (based on Luis Muñoz Marín, governor of Puerto Rico 1948–1964), who at one time condemned colonialism and the exploitation that Puerto Rico suffered at the hands of the United States,[14] undergoes a change of heart toward the liberty of his island. Marqués believes that this change results from self-interest — the governor's fear that his power would be diminished in a free Puerto Rico. His abil-ity to act for the collective welfare of the nation is undermined when he places personal ambition above the nation's destiny.

In the presence of Teresias, a poet and friend of the governor, Don José's wife Doña Isabel recalls her husband's youthful ideals:

One day three unknown men came to the mountain: you Teresias; Alberto's father [Alberto is the fiancé of the governor's daughter Casandra]; and Joseph. The poet, the philosopher, and the politician.[15] Three men intent on the noble task of saving a nation. Don Rodrigo [Albizu Campos] had begun to serve his imprisonment in the United States. And you had decided that his sacrifice should not be in vain. Moreover, to the ideal of political liberty for the colony you had added the ideals of social reform and democratic life for the nation. For two years you had marched through valleys and mountains as three Wise Men of a new Epiphany, offering to the nation the three gifts of an ancient wisdom: land, bread, emancipation.

(...un día llegaron a la montaña tres desconocidos: usted, Teresias; el padre de Alberto; y José. El poeta, el filósofo y el político. Tres hombres empeñados en la noble tarea de redimir a un pueblo. Don Rodrigo había empezado a cumplir su larga condena en el Norte. Y ustedes habían decidido que su sacrificio no fuese en vano. Más aún, al ideal de libertad política para la colonia añadían los ideales de reforma social y vida democrática para el pueblo. Por dos años habían marchado los tres por valles y montañas como Tres Magos de una nueva Epifanía, ofrendando al pueblo los tres dones de una sabiduría milenaria: agro, pan, emancipación.)[16]

The three men all proceed to realize their ideals. But when Don José attains power, he stresses "bread" or economic security, which involves continued dependency on the United States. He knows that the masses prize material benefits — high salaries, new industries fostered by the U.S.; in turn, they respect the leadership of the man who is instrumental in providing them with these assets. Don José refuses to heed warnings from friends and relatives who remind him of his failure to follow through by advancing toward political freedom after obtaining economic security. He battles Don Rodrigo's ideal of independence (the man has recently returned to the island) by means of espionage and the revival of an old anti-subversive law for use against the man and his followers. Don José also hastens the signing of the Commonwealth, in order to solidify ties with the United States.

Throughout the drama, Marqués underscores the "unnatural" coexistence of Don José and his island. The governor himself is portrayed as an insincere, rhetorical politician, as a giant in a government of dwarfs. Marqués also characterizes palace officials as automatons, petty bourgeoise who lack vision or thought.

Under Don José's regime, nature is either absent or destroyed: the nightingale flees at the sound of Don José's voice; his daughter

Casandra dreams that she cuts down the ceiba tree because the nightingale no longer sings. The ideal of liberation, depicted in the drama as a seed, is not to be allowed to flower. In one scene, Doña Isabel is unable to convince her husband to permit the seed to germinate in order that the country may once more have life and roots. The unnatural state of the world ruled by Don José is communicated by his refusal to believe that a natural disaster will befall Puerto Rico. He tells Teresias:

Do you believe that there will be a storm this year?.... A cyclon has not whipped us for more than twenty years.... Even the blind forces of nature are propitious to us. Doesn't that tell you anything, visionary?

(¿Crees que habrá tormenta este año?... Hace más de veinte años que no nos azota un ciclón.... Hasta las fuerzas ciegas de la naturaleza nos son propicias. ¿No te dice nada eso, visionario? [II, 260–61].)

Marqués invests this statement with political overtones; he emphasizes Don José's limited vision, his blindness to the growing political (and for Marqués, "natural") torment that will cause his death.

This storm accumulates force with an attack on the governor's palace and a nationalist attempt to take over some of the island towns. After suppressing this insurrection, Don José makes clear his intention to sign the protectorate with the United States. The eye of the storm approaches quickly: Alberto renounces his government position and plans to assassinate Don José. When Casandra discovers the revolver he carries, she struggles with him, and Alberto is killed when the gun accidentally fires. These events take place in the festive atmosphere of the reception at which the protectorate will be signed.

The spotlight now focuses on Casandra, whose rebellion against her father has been brewing throughout the drama. At the outset of the play Casandra clings to an idyllic vision of life and of her love for Alberto and for her family. Her world is "ordered," filled with love and happiness both in the personal and political realms. Her perspective soon broadens. Even before the nationalist attack on the palace, she senses disorder when her father, fearing Don Rodrigo, confines her in the palace under heavy guard. She relates all this to Don José's struggle to maintain his power. She discovers that her father's egotism endangers the country and begins to equate the North American way of life, symbolized by the protectorate, with death for Puerto Rico. The daughter's rebellion reaches its dramatic conclusion at the reception, where she kills her father and herself.[17] Marqués associates Casandra with the Lord's justice: she becomes immortalized in marble in the denouement, with her hand raised to symbolize the blow she has dealt to try to right the moral order.

Marqués' portrayal of the character Don José is complex. He endows the "villain" Don José with some positive qualities that arouse our sympathy. He also attributes to him the eyes of a poet, not those of a politician. These qualities make Don José at least theoretically capable of Teresias' poetic vision.[18] Sensitive to the need for family solidarity, he tells his wife, "Without you I am always alone" (Sin ti estoy siempre a solas" [I, 214]). When Don José learns of espionage against Don Rodrigo, his instinctive reaction is negative, although he recognizes Don Rodrigo's threat to the status quo. Aware of his own growing insensitivity, he compares his lack of consciousness to that of a spider that he sees in his office. At least on an intellectual level, he perceives the beginning of his downfall. He speaks of Alberto's father, who refused a government post because he feared that power would corrupt his ideals. Don José realizes that idealism comes easily before one attains power: "It is easy to be everything before obtaining power" ("Es fácil serlo todo antes de llegar al poder" [I, 234]). Yet his distillation of the essential human condition is at the same time a rationalization of human behavior. Don José knows that power corrupts, but isolates himself in his lonely battle to maintain power. He relinquishes the channels of communication with others that would help to determine the needs of the people.

It is precisely this lack of evolution that is criticized by D. L. Shaw,[19] who argues that Don José's tragic essence is undermined by the fact that his momentary flashes of insight lead to no decision — or rather a decision that contradicts his insights. But one must bear in mind that Don José is modeled after Luis Muñoz Marín — Marqués' "villain" who betrayed his island's aspirations for liberty. Marqués does not wish to arouse excessive sympathy for this man, for he wants to specify his historic error. He is willing to invest Don José with some sensitivity, but wishes to demonstrate how Don José rejects this sensitivity, consciously choosing to become a self-serving politician.

Marqués shows a different kind of evolution in Casandra — a positive evolution that also serves Marqués' thesis. Casandra moves toward the world of ideals; Marqués anticipates her moral development. At the outset, Casandra is a naive girl, oblivious to her country's problems. She jokingly toasts Don Rodrigo — anticipating her later acceptance of his ideals. Gradually discovering her father's egotistical motivation, she becomes disillusioned. Alberto wisely counsels her that she must no longer pattern herself after the image of her father; she must destroy it and forge her own image of life. Alberto's advice anticipates her literal parricide in the denouement. Casandra has not yet formulated definite ideals. But her mother advises her to maintain faith in Alberto and his ideals. And after Alberto's death, these ideals thrive in Casandra. She becomes Marqués' model Puerto Rican, who not only believes in a cause, but is willing to sacrifice herself for it.

Death Shall Not Enter the Palace manifests sophistication in its portrayal of interrelationships. In *The Oxcart,* for example, Juanita's growth is hastened by her experiences in New York. Secondary, rather than central, characters help foster Juanita's awareness of the plight of the emigrant Puerto Rican and that of other minority groups living in the metropolis. In *Death Shall Not Enter the Palace,* in contrast, central characters interact to foster Casandra's development. The characters' interaction in the drama revolves about the conflict between personal and national obligations.

Although sociopolitical, the play has universal overtones. Don José's actions constitute an infringement of the moral order, and in varying degrees — from attempts at persuasion to outright assassination[20] — steps are taken to restore moral order. A fusion of religious symbols and elements from classical Greek tragedy keep the play on this universal plane. A Greek chorus chants the words love, pain, misery; stock tragic characters appear — including Tiresias of *Oedipus Rex* and Casandra of *Agamemnon* and the *Trojan Women,* two visionary characters whose prophecies are traditionally disbelieved. Casandra, though, is more than a prophetess of doom here, for she enacts her father's "doom" in the denouement. Stage effects include a Great Voice (or the voice of Don Rodrigo) citing passages from the Bible. Puerto Rico is compared to a house built on false foundations that will crumble when the Lord enacts his vengeance. The same voices anticipate the scenes of love, pain, and misery, which are necessary to restore moral order.

In this work, Marqués intensifies the use of lighting, music, and sound effects. He uses a blue or bright light to signify ideals (the blue light over Casandra in the denouement). Red light illuminates

Casandra just before her bloody sacrifice. "Unreal," wierd music serves as the leitmotif whenever Marqués wishes to signal ideals; it is heard when Don Rodrigo arrives at the airport. It is also played at the outset, when the Great Voice lets Teresias see the future — in which justice will be enacted so that ideals may survive. Dramatic music serves as a transition between scenes and recurs at highly epic moments. The solemn tone suggested by the biblical passages is intensified by religious music, especially when Casandra is seen praying before the reception. Music also provides contrast: the melodic festivity of the reception clashes with Alberto's tragic death in the foreground. As in *Juan Bobo,* the blues are heard when the American — the commissioner from the North — arrives at the reception to sign the protectorate.

Blackouts are used frequently, and events are simulated by sounds alone. For example, during the attack on the palace, enacted in total darkness, we hear the siren, the voice of Don Rodrigo, the song of the nightingale and tropical insects, the screeching of the auto, the machine gun fire, and the cries of Don José: "They want to kill me" ("Quieren matarme" [I, 255], which anticipates his assassination). The airport scene is also enacted in darkness: the audience hears the landing of the plane, the voices of arriving passengers and customs' officials, the protest of one woman who is not allowed to bring a plant into the country, and the dramatic resistance of Don Rodrigo who brings into the country the "seed" of liberty. The blackout facilitates the transition to the next scene and permits Marqués to manipulate time: Six months have passed, and Don José's nervous tirade reveals that Don Rodrigo's seed has indeed germinated on the Island.

As in *The Sun and the MacDonalds,* Marqués makes use of the flashback. Yet *Death Shall Not Enter the Palace* is more innovative; the play opens with the denouement: we see the marble figure of Casandra and the image of Teresias, who envisions this "future." He informs us that the scene we are witnessing is yet to happen; the curtain then rises on a complete flashback of the events that lead up to this finale.

As with *Juan Bobo,* the political implications of *Death Shall Not Enter the Palace* have overridden its artistic qualities in the public's eye. Censorship has been levied against the drama in Puerto Rico, and it has never been produced. Despite the passing of many years since the termination of Muñoz Marín's governorship, the pro-commonwealth Popular Democratic party continues to avoid criticism of its ideology even in the guise of art. Whether the play will ever be valued for its artistic element alone remains to be seen.

IV   Un niño azul para esa sombra
(A Blue Child for that Shadow)

In *A Blue Child for that Shadow* (1958),[21] Marqués portrays the comfortable elite and intelligentsia of Puerto Rico and dramatizes their perspectives on the island's economy and political character. As in *The Eve of Manhood,* Marqués examines the formation of a child's perspective in a world that offers discrepant views on society and man's place within it. In the novel, Pirulo early encounters conflicting attitudes as he moves away from the nuclear family; in the play the child Michelín absorbs disparate perspectives within the family unit: his materialistic, Americanized mother, Mercedes, conflicts with his revolutionary father, Michel. Marqués dramatizes the child's intense identification with his father's world and his pathetic attempt to resist his mother's world. The struggle leads to the boy's severe frustration and eventually to suicide.

Marqués signals the destruction of the child's universe in several symbolic steps. Michelín's father — model for the child's ideals — is absent from the home: Judged guilty for his participation in a revolutionary uprising, Michel is condemned to a prison term of eight years. During the father's imprisonment, Michelín makes a father image of the *quenepo* tree on the patio; the tree seems to have the father's strength and roots. But Mercedes poisons the tree to enlarge the terrace, so that it will accommodate more people at her cocktail parties. No sooner does Michel return from jail, than he rapidly leaves home again: the knowledge of his wife's adultery during his absence disgusts him. Michelín is left once again without the model he needs so desperately to reinforce the conviction that others — family, friends, teachers — are trying to deny. Michelín is now forced to summon his father in dreams, retreating into a fantasy world. Believing that his father has gone to Chile, Michelín respects him for helping oppressed mine workers. Yet even Michelín's dream is destroyed: Mercedes reveals that his father never went to Chile, but rather to New York, where he died, a disillusioned, bitter man, on a bench in Washington Square.

Michelín's own suicide follows: symbolically he is "un niño azul" — the blue light of idealism living a tenuous existence in a society that accepts the shadow, or *sombra,* of North American domination. The idealistic child can never mature in such an environment, for his ideals have no basis in reality. He has no real model for resistance — only the distorted vision of his absent father. When his mother deflates Michelín's ideal, he retreats deeper into his dream world, seeking physical as well as emotional escape. In this drama Marqués intensifies the significance of the color blue; it is associated not only with dreams and ideals, but also with death: the bottle containing the poison (which was also used to kill the *quenepo*) is blue; and one of Michelín's friends, Andrés, who witnesses the boy's death, notes that Michelín turns blue after he drinks the venom.

A *Blue Child for that Shadow* represents a landmark in Marqués' development as a dramatist. It is poetic drama that integrates lyrical passages and explicit symbolism into a dramatic setting, especially in the scenes that depict Michelín's fantasy. For example, Michelín frequently relives the scene of the poisoning of the *quenepo* tree with Cecilia, a woman who was raised with Michel and who came to live with Mercedes and Michelín after Michel's imprisonment. Marqués has the boy climb a trellis, positioning himself for recollection of the traumatic sight: he imagines his mother pouring the poison over the tree's roots. Afterwards, we see the child pathetically descend, leaving behind the lost ideal.

Marqués perfects stage devices used earlier. The familiar flashback technique becomes more innovative: Act I shows the present — Michelín's constant tension with his mother; Act II goes back two years to explain the tensions of the present; Act III picks up from Act I, as if there were no interruption, and leads to the tragic denouement. Marqués also uses flashbacks within flashbacks — a carryover from the novel *The Eve of Manhood:* in Act II, Michel recalls the attack of the revolutionaries and his court conviction, while sound effects and music suggest these events.

Death Shall Not Enter the Palace used sound effects to indicate a chronological sequence in time. They are used more innovatively in *A Blue Child,* in conjunction with visual elements, to reflect the movement of time within a flashback. After Michel's condemnation, Marqués presents a farewell scene between Mercedes and Michel. In the background a song about false oaths is heard — ironic anticipation of Mercedes' adultery. One then hears the cry of a baby (Michelín) that immediately turns into the cries of several older children — schoolmates who years later taunt Michelín, calling his father an assassin, subversive, and traitor.

Visual and auditory elements — Cecilia's song of the death of a child, Michelín's pose as a crucified victim when he climbs the trellis, the bottle of poison — are scattered throughout the play and anticipate the denouement. These elements are also recollected poetically in the final scene. The drama demonstrates Marqués' growing mastery in the use of visual and auditory effects. In the scene of the child's discovery of his mother's adultery, a single object — a bouncing ball — is paramount and provides a subtle symbolism. At the beginning of the scene, one hears Michelín's ball bouncing outside. When the telephone rings, Michelín answers and then calls his mother. Michelín is told to go play on the terrace. While his mother is conversing with Philip, the ball bounces into the room. We see Michelín enter on tiptoe to retrieve the ball at precisely the moment when Mercedes breaks off her relationship with Philip. Michelín's eyes open wide, and he immediately manifests a coldness toward his mother. The ball takes us through an emotionally charged scene. An object of the child's world, it also plays a major role in Michelín's loss of naiveté.

A Blue Child for that Shadow is not only outstanding for its stylistic innovations, but also for the complexity of its characters. With the revelation of the father's unheroic end, Marqués goes beyond political rhetoric to add another dimension to the drama. It is no longer a simple defense of liberation efforts and the critique of Americanization. Michel's complexity as a character becomes evident. He makes a heroic choice, but his commitment seems to be mixed with vanity. Cecilia pleads with him to remain with the family as a protector. Michel admits that he cannot face the sacrifice that this would entail; to remain in Puerto Rico would mean his exposure as a social pariah to his son and as a man kept by a rich, adulterous wife. He leaves to save face and sells out — emigrating to America, the country theoretically held responsible for his island's enslaved condition. In his essay "The Docile Puerto Rican," Marqués judged the actions of this character as those of a weak, if not docile, man who brings about only destruction — his own and his son's.

The "villainess" Mercedes is also presented as a complex character. Marqués does not discount the sufferings she experienced as the wife of a political prisoner: society repudiated her husband's actions; children taunted her son at school; she was cut off by her own banker brothers, who feared association with the wife of a revolutionary. Like her husband, she was victimized by society's prejudices. She had admired and tolerated, but not shared, her husband's ideals. Michel evolved from professor to revolutionary very quickly, and Mercedes was not prepared for her new role as the wife of a revolutionary. Pained at rejection by a world she has always known and loved, she tries to win back a place in that world, endorsing the status quo and destroying her husband's "subversive" manuscripts. Her actions are horrendous, yet comprehensible, in a society that ostracizes the dissenter. Unlike the politician Don José, who betrays ideals, Mercedes never belonged to the world of ideals. Her actions seem natural and inevitable. Her nobility sometimes outweighs Michel's: while she sacrifices her lover to preserve home and family, Michel sacrifices his family to pursue his struggle for liberty. The roles of hero and villain become increasingly ambiguous in the play, for ultimately society is the primary cause of a frazzled marriage, emotional ravagement, and finally death. Marqués offers no clear solution.

A Blue Child for that Shadow is definitely an artful drama in which Marqués' stylistic inventory is perfected. He draws on these stage devices in later work, at the same time that he continues to experiment with different literary trends.

V   La casa sin reloj (The House Without a Clock)

In *The House Without a Clock* (1960), Marqués focuses on yet another segment of Puerto Rican society, the bourgeoisie, contrasting its political complacency with the concerned activism of the nationalists. As in his earlier plays, Marqués depicts this corner of society within a family setting — in this case concentrating on the relationship between two brothers, Pedro and José. At the same time, he depicts the political consciousness raising of one member of the bourgeoisie — Pedro's wife Micaela.

Marqués explores the emerging middle class, which is exemplified by Pedro, a forty-four-year old government employee who typifies devotion to the material, colonial world created by his government under the aegis of the United States. He refuses to see beyond the limits of his own existence and even refuses to acknowledge his brother because they disagree on economic and political issues. Pedro feels comfortable with his role as a colonized Puerto Rican who conforms to the status quo. Identifying with his likeminded countrymen, he says, "My brothers are those who think as I do,..." ("Mis hermanos son los que piensan como yo,...").[22]

He has filtered this attitude to his son, who represents the future bourgeoisie and who will never reject the world passed on to him in order to create a new structure for the nation. We learn from Micaela that their son only thinks about money, that he studies economics during the day and business administration at night. The idealistic brother, José, suffers for his attempts to change the humdrum, bourgeois world. Suspected by the police of subversive activity, he hides in Pedro's house. His interaction with Micaela is instrumental in awakening her guilt at the nation's plight.

Despite this hopeful aspect of *The House Without a Clock,* Marqués portrays his society as absurd. He adopts many elements of the Theater of the Absurd to convey his political and humanistic orientation.[23] In keeping with the aims of this genre, Marqués projects his own reaction to the world around him[24] by exposing what he sees as unauthentic ways of life. Marqués wishes for his countrymen to face the absurdity of their enslaved condition[25] in terms of both political and ethical values.

Setting the stage for his commentary, Marqués furnishes the house in an absurd fashion imported from the States. Why stuff vases with artificial flowers in a tropical culture where natural flowers bloom year round? Why place a tea or coffee table in the living room? Puerto Ricans never drink tea, except when they have stomach trouble, and they always drink coffee in the dining room. Marqués ironically explains the coffee table's function: it is a resting place for unpaid bills.

Marqués also points out the falsity of a static society, which allows no possibility for change. In such a world, time loses meaning. When Micaela speaks to the "wrong number" on the telephone, she learns that the party has thirteen clocks, but still does not know what hour it is. The play's title, "The House Without a Clock," reflects the fact that Micaela has no timepiece in her house.

Within this dateless society, Marqués points out the absurdity of efforts to prevent change — specifically, the persecution of the nationalist. Police are given the right to enter homes without a search warrant to apprehend nationalists who threaten the status quo. The police violate civil rights and expect people like Micaela to inform on any nationalist attempt or thought. Once denounced and arrested, the nationalist cannot count on legal assistance. Marqués portrays an island pervaded by fear of disruption of the status quo and, after an attack on the governor's palace, controlled by the military. He notes that nationalists who clearly have no direct responsibility for a particular disruption are nevertheless arrested. José insists that he is persecuted even though he has not carried out a single nationalist act. In this society, one is found guilty by association, in "a type of complicity by remote control" ("Una especie de complicidad por control remoto" [I, 54]).

Marqués' view of the absurd economic and political situation of his island is translated into a dramatic image of a truly absurd society in an effort to shock his bourgeois audience.[26] In the tradition of Pinter, Marqués stresses the impossibility of unraveling human motivations. Elements of the absurd pervade Micaela's actions and attitudes. She habitually forgets to cook for her husband. She accepts the lack of solidarity between husband and wife and considers it normal for her husband to have a girlfriend. Adultery is no tragedy here as it is in *A Blue Child,* and Micaela even goes to the trouble of selecting furniture for Pedro's mistress. No one in this setting has a clear sense of purpose. The detective who questions Micaela is soon distracted by the "escape" novel she is reading; *La hora del amor (The Hour of Love)* is more absorbing than his "duty" to prosecute nationalists.

Verbal nonsense, learned from Beckett, Adamov, and Ionesco, reflects the paucity of communication between human beings[27] and dominates the play's disjointed conversations. When José kisses Micaela, all emotion is reduced to a statistical count of the number of kisses each has received in a lifetime. Micaela accounts for one of these statistics, describing how she was kissed by a school principal when she was a teacher and how she left the school. José logically assumes that she left because of this incident, but she informs him that in fact she had developed an unfortunate allergy to chalk dust; and when one is sneezing, it is impossible to kiss. This comic lack of communication, of course, parallels the more serious lack of communication between José and his brother.

Marqués' characterization of Micaela is quite subtle. Representing the absurd, she also personifies man's exit from the absurd. The audience's initial impression of her as a harried, unthinking housewife gives way to the portrait of a woman concerned with political and ethical issues. To effect this, Marqués has Micaela accept the absurd world. In keeping with Albert Camus' insistence, in *The Myth of Sisyphus,* that to face life means to accept its absurd nature,[28] Micaela tells us that happiness consists of changing the

preposterous nature of the world or "accepting the absurd nature
of the world, naturally, as if one does not recognize its absurdity"
("aceptar lo absurdo que es el mundo con naturalidad tal, como si
no se percibiera su . . . absurdidad" [I, 48]). She accepts a world in
which a deafening radio strings together advertising jingles and
bulletins reporting the arrest of nationalists, making no distinction
as to the degree of seriousness of one or the other. Her acceptance
of the absurd mechanization of human interaction is reflected in
the following conversation:

> Hello! Hello!
> (Pause)
> No sir, this is not the operator. You have the wrong number.
> (Pause)
> You're welcome. Don't worry! I am accustomed to the absurdity of
> these automatic telephone connections.

> (¡Aló! Aló!
> [Pausa]
> No, señor, no es la central. Se ha equivocado de número.
> [Pausa]
> No hay de qué. ¡Figúrese! Ya estoy acostumbrada a los absurdos de
> estas conexiones automáticas [I, 14]).

Micaela's acceptance of life's inanity enables her to recognize
and pinpoint the absurdity of other people's beliefs. When Pedro
unreasonably blames José's nationalism for their mother's death —
"If you had been a good son, you would not have become a
nationalist. You would not have done it, knowing the ailment of
our poor mother" ("Si hubieras sido un buen hijo, no te habrías
hecho nacionalista. No lo habrías hecho, sabiendo la dolencia de
nuestra pobre madre"), José shouts indignantly, "Imbecile! Do
you think that a man chooses his ideals according to the ailments of
his family?" ("¡Imbécil! ¿Crees que un hombre va a escoger sus
ideales de acuerdo con las enfermedades de la familia?" [II, 70]).
At this point, Micaela intervenes with comical Logic: "Pedro, I believe that josé is right. Take youself as an example. Do you Remember? Last year I had a stomach operation, and you did not stop being a member of the government party" ("Pedro, creo que José
tiene razón. Tú mismo, toma por caso. ¿Recuerdas? El año pasado
a mí me hicieron una operación de vientry y tú no dejaste de ser
miembro del partido de gobierno [II, 70–71]). When Pedro, at the
boiling point, wants to know how her stomach is connected with

party membership, Micaela calmly answers: in the same way that his mother's illness is connected with José's nationalism.

Pedro's absurdity lies in his acceptance of only those associations that preserve his reality. Micaela, on the other hand, is willing to see connections and ideas not admitted by others. Though her own ideas are sometimes illogical, she learns by examining various perspectives; she recreates a world for herself by juggling perspectives and associations freely.[29] This is her response to a structure that disallows change. And this response enables her to escape the confines of her husband's world and, through an acceptance of the absurd, to create a logical structure in which to assimilate some of José's world. Not wanting to be like the transparent Pedro who fears dignity, spirit, and truth, she wants to experience change. She and José discuss the terms "nation," "liberty," and "guilt complex"; she perceives that José's guilt complex stems "from knowing that your nation lives without the liberty that you wish for it. And you have to pay for this lack, . . . on behalf of those who are not even conscious of their guilt. And you pay for them by being a nationalist. . . . You are a generous man, José. I am not" ("de saber que su pueblo vive sin la libertad que usted para él ansia. Y usted tiene que pagar por esa falta de su pueblo, . . . por los que no tienen siquiera conciencia de la culpa. Y lo paga usted siendo nacionalista. . . . Usted es un ser generoso, José. Yo, yo no lo soy" [II, 75]).

Micaela wishes to become "generous" — to assume a guilt complex over her island's plight. To effect this, she kills José — embodiment of ideals. This absurd ending is actually in keeping with Marqués' political orientation. The destruction of ideals should instill in man an intense sense of guilt. In the denouement, Marqués presents a Micaela who is relieved that her guilt is finally concrete. This scene is designed to shock Marqués' audience into seeing the absurdity of Puerto Ricans who destroy independence ideals without experiencing any guilt. Micaela transgresses in order to assume the guilt that others should also assume. She then enters the world of time, and Marqués tells us: "A clock is heard striking the hour, as the curtain falls very rapidly" ("Se oye un reloj de campana dar la hora, mientras cae muy rápido el telón" [II, 120]).

Micaela has a sense of humor; the spontaneity she shares with José becomes an important ingredient in the play, balancing direct political rhetoric. Timing is crucial to this humor: it is not until Act II that Micaela and José finally introduce themselves by name, though they have spent Act I baring their souls to each other. José's telephone conversation with Pedro's mistress is also highly comical:

Pedro can't come to the phone. He's not dressed.
  (Pause)
Lady, aren't you ashamed?
  (Pause)
Not here, in the bedroom with his wife.
  (Irritated)
No, she is not nude!
  (Perturbed)
That is, I don't know.
  (Uneasy, he looks toward the door on the right)
At least she had on clothes when she entered the room.

(Pedro no puede venir. Esá desnudo.
  [Pausa]
Señora, ¿no tiene usted vergüenza?
  [Pausa]
Aquí no, en la habitación, con su mujer.
  [Irritado]
¡No, ella no está desnuda!
  [Perturbado]
Digo, no sé
  [Inquieto, mira hacia la puerta de la derecha]
Por lo menos tenía ropa al entrar [II, 89–90].)

Marqués also treats problems of the modern world — mechanization and the trap of easy credit — with the same humor. Wrong numbers multiply until José inevitably reaches the "wrong number" that had previously called Micaela. When José, wishing to escape from the island, asks Pedro to buy him passage on a plane, Pedro replies that he has no money. Micaela responds: "And what do you want money for? Our life is an eternal credit" ("¿Y para qué quieres dinero? Nuestra vida es un eterno crédito" [II, 99]). When Pedro informs her that he has exhausted his credit, Micaela plays with words, declaring that the more discredited his credit, the more credit he can receive.

In *The House Without a Clock,* Marqués employs a transition between acts, reminiscent of the technique employed by Miguel de Cervantes in the episode of Don Quijote and the Biscayan (*vizcaíno*). At the end of Act or "Absurd" I, the curtain drops abruptly on Pedro and José as they recognize each other. Pedro says only "You!" and the audience does not yet know that they are brothers. Act II opens as if no time has passed. Pedro repeats the word "You!" and the action proceeds. (Don Quijote and the Biscayan raise their swords at the end of one chapter, and the fight proceeds at the outset of another.)

In the tradition of Desnos' "Antipoème" and Ionesco's "antipièce," Marqués labeled his drama as "an antipoetic comedy in two absurdities and a reasonable finale" ("Comedia antipoética en dos absurdos y un final razonable" [p. 5]). But he did not adopt the devices of the Theater of the Absurd wholesale; he did not altogether rule out character development or plot. Marqués further deviates from the genre by infusing a social message into his work. As Esslin notes, "The Theater of the Absurd, . . . which proceeds not by intellectual concepts but by poetic images, neither poses an intellectual problem in its exposition nor provides any clear-cut solution that would be reducible to a lesson or apophthegm."[30] Marqués proposes solutions to society's problems, implying the possibility of change through political consciousness raising.

VI   Mariana o el alba (Mariana, or the Dawn)

In *Mariana, or the Dawn* (1965), Marqués traces the fall of an 1868 revolutionary movement against Spanish colonization of Puerto Rico, a movement commonly known as "El Grito de Lares" ("The Cry of Lares").[31] The author attributes the failure of this uprising to the human shortcoming that, in his view, has dominated twentieth century politics — the primacy of individual self-interest. Marqués fixes on the betrayal of one Puerto Rican, who chooses money over his island's freedom.

The attempted uprising at Lares had already been dramatized by the poet Luis Lloréns Torres in *Grito de Lares* (1914).[32] Lloréns Torres romanticized the figure of the country peasant Manolo; Marqués features Mariana Bracetti de Rojas as the heroine of his drama. Mariana is the wife of revolutionary leader Manuel Rojas — a wealthy landowner originally from Venezuela. History records that Mariana Bracetti de Rojas, a valiant revolutionary who embroidered the flag of Lares, was imprisoned after the defeat of the revolution; while in jail, she gave birth to a stillborn child, an event that Marqués uses as a symbol of the aborted revolution.

In this drama, events move swiftly to the tragic finale. Suspense is created at the outset with the planning of the revolution, and the stress is placed on the conspirators' grave danger. At a reception given by Mariana and her husband, to which "enemy" Spaniards are invited, Marqués expertly contrasts the revolutionaries' outward frivolity and humor with their inner tensions. Marqués also portrays the internal odds against the revolutionaries. Not all countrymen understand and accept revolutionary ideals; there is much impatience, passion, and impetuosity to launch headlong into the insurrection. The odds against the conspirators increase when their leader is exiled.[33] There are no assured reinforcements; the small band is undisciplined. The authorities begin to arrest suspicious individuals, but the insurrection begins anyway, prompted by discontent and fear of espionage.[34] Perhaps one of the best scenes in the play is the revolutionaries' march to Lares, which becomes a dramatic spectacle, accompanied by the sound of prayers and choral singing and illuminated by torchlight. Triumphant at Lares, the revolutionary troops are betrayed at San Sebastián del Pepino. Marqués stages the disastrous divisiveness among islanders: Reinaldo Domenech, a native Puerto Rican, informs the authorities of the revolutionary activities of Mariana and her co-conspirators, exchanging the spiritual independence of his island for material gain. Mariana's words seem to convey Marqués' own bitterness at the sell out:

For money, then! You have sold youself like ... a common prostitute. (With a terrible voice) And do you know that others poorer than Reinaldo Domenech, men, women and children who have suffered hunger, who have never been able to wear a pair of shoes in their lives, are now, at this moment, falling, dying, beneath Spanish bullets in San Sebastián del Pepino?... On account of you! Do you realize, miserable man, that you have destroyed this people's opportunity to be free?... Coward!

(¡Por dinero, entonces! Se ha vendido usted como ... una vulgar ramera. [Con voz terrible.] ¿Y sabe usted que otros más pobres que Reinaldo Domenech, hombres, mujeres y casi niños que han pasado hambre, quienes jamás han podido usar un par de zapatos en sus vidas, están ahora, en estos momentos, cayendo, muriendo, bajo las balas españolas en San Sebastián del Pepino?... ¡Por usted! ¿Se da cuenta, miserable, de que ha destruido la oportunidad de este pueblo a ser libre?... ¡Cobarde! [II, 179].)

This tirade is also directed at those twentieth century traitors who barter Puerto Rican independence for material gain.

Imprisoned by Mariana, Domenech manages to escape, but he is ultimately killed. Mariana's husband is eventually captured, and Mariana is jailed. For Mariana, there is no end to the tragedy. She is separated from her husband, and her child is stillborn. The persecution of the revolutionary is devastating, but Marqués' presentation is not without hope. In an effort to inspire his countrymen on the centennial of this insurrection, Marqués wrote a play that dramatizes tremendous revolutionary zeal. When the disillusioned Miguel returns home in defeat, Mariana assures him that this is only a setback; the ideal lives on, and the aspirations of martyred revolutionaries must be pursued by those who remain. Mariana, sentenced to prison, tells her adopted daughter Rosaura that she must never abandon the cause for which she and Miguel sacrificed themselves. Mariana has fulfilled her obligation to herself and her island; others must carry on in her place.

Revolutionary zeal is not the only positive feature of the drama. Marqués offers an extensive description of Puerto Rican culture: music and dance are important elements in the play. The characters communicate their ties with the land — its coffee plantations and blossoming fruit and flowers, its mountains of different hues of green. When Mariana bids farewell to Rosaura, making her guardian of the estate, she says, "The estate must never be sold. Not to anyone. At any price. Land is the Puerto Ricans' only heritage. It must always be ours. Always!" ("La hacienda no se venderá jamás. A nadie, a ningún precio. La tierra es el único patrimonio de los puertorriqueños. Deberá ser nuestra siempre. ¡Siempre!" [II, 207].)

In the context of one nineteenth century family, in *Mariana* Marqués depicts the Puerto Rican racial unity that is absent in the twentieth century. This racial unity transcends socioeconomic barriers. The white *jíbaro* Santiago and the mulatto Redención teach Rosaura to play the *bordonúa* (an oversized guitar that produces a solemn sound). The bond between races is also manifested in the tender love between Redención and Rosaura.[35]

The playwright places on Mariana's desk Manuel Alonso's book, *El gíbaro* (The Jibaro or Peasant), which defines the Puerto Rican in terms of indigenous values. Other books on Mariana's desk include *El cerco de Numancia (The Siege of Numancia)* by Miguel de Cervantes, the story of a town whose populace chooses mass suicide rather than submit to Roman domination. Puerto Rican religion and art are present in Mariana's home, represented by the picture of the country's patron saint — the Virgin of Providence. This sense of solidarity, of cultural roots, and of resistance to domination is the liberation that Marqués desires for his island. The author also wishes for the majority to internalize the tremendous faith exemplified by Mariana as she walks out of prison at the end of the drama, carrying her dead child in her arms. She predicts that future generations will be born in the shadow of enslavement, but believes in an eventual utopia that will see the "radiant sun of liberty" ("el sol radiante de la libertad" [III, 238]). A guard's remark about the coldness of the dawn contrasts with Mariana's determined optimism. The morning may indeed be cold, but the "light" of the sun symbolically follows Mariana as the curtain falls.

Mariana, or the Dawn, which bears resemblances to García Lorca's *Mariana Pineda,* tends to be more heavyhanded than the dramatic works that preceded it. Marqués' sense of mission generates an abundance of political clichés. The play's fabric of symbolism is not subtle, woven as it is to clothe Marqués' political message. For example, during the insurrection, the country's "death" in colonization is symbolized by a flag whose black letters spell out "Patria." In contrast, the hoped for resurrection of the nation is signified by white letters that spell "liberty." Two political emblems — the island "Flower of Passion" ("Flor de la Pasión"), also called the Flower of Redemption, and the Spanish officer's sword — are utilized with a rather obvious irony: When Beatriz offers the island flower to the Spanish officer, he accepts, with ironic lack of awareness, a symbol of Puerto Rican redemption and liberty. The Spaniard is also made to politely, and again ironically, "surrender" his sword to Mariana, who, at a dinner, acts as the perfect hostess and helps the Spanish officer to "disarm."

Mention should be made of "censorship" in this play — this time, not society's suppression of the drama, but Marqués' own censorship within the play. In a prologue to the drama, the editor notes that Marqués faithfully renders the language, folklore, architecture, dress, furniture, and customs of the epoch.[36] But Marqués does recast historical events to suit his political purposes. His relentless anti-Americanism prevents him from dramatizing American participation in the Lares revolution: the North American Matthew Bruckman was a martyr of the uprising. Luis Lloréns Tores dramatizes Bruckman's heroism, expressing his nationalist sentiments in nongrammatical Spanish:

No importance that my death
to be for a foreign country.
Thus, to bequeath great fame
To my race and my nation.

(No importancia que mi muerte
ser por país extranjero.
Así legar grande fama
a mi raza y a mi pueblo [II, 105].)

Marqués discounts Bruckman's role, even distorting his name. On more than one occasion we hear of a certain Burgman who is gathering forces for the revolution. Did the editor simply misprint the name — repeatedly? Marqués recognizes only one American ideal — money. Mariana learns that the American who sells arms to the revolutionaries doubles his price. In this instance, Marqués acts as a censor, rewriting history to suit his own ideological bent.

Marqués' social drama — *The Oxcart, Juan Bobo and the Lady of the Occident, Death Shall Not Enter the Palace, A Blue Child for that Shadow, The House Without a Clock, Mariana, or the Dawn* — contains the history of Puerto Rican dependency, first under Spain and then under the United States. Drawing on a variety of dramatic techniques and genres, Marqués stages both a social critique and a kind of political wishfulfillment. In these plays, Marqués' dramatic development is consistent, reaching its peak in *A Blue Child for that Shadow*. His next production sees him absorbed in the Theater of the Absurd. *Mariana* contains politics and melodrama, which serve Marqués' thesis well, but at the same time undermine his art.

In the next chapter, we shall analyze a group of Marqués' dramas that we will label social-existential. The scene may still be placed within a social context, Puerto Rico's problems may still be exposed; yet what in some cases becomes more salient are the existential themes of time, man's essence and circumstances, as well as the problems of modern society.

CHAPTER 8

Social-Existential Drama

I   Los soles truncos (The Truncated Suns)

IN *The Truncated Suns* (1958), Marqués delves into the relationships among three elderly sisters who share an old house in San
Juan. One sister, Hortensia, has just died; her body lies in another
room during the action of the play, and she is revived in the imagi-
nations of the other two sisters. The women dwell exclusively in the
past, remembering their papa, Burkhart, a German naturalist who
came to the tropics and became the owner of an estate, and their
mother, the beautiful Andalusian with the Grecian beauty — her
hair dark and thick as the wine of Málaga.[1] Educated in Europe,
the sisters slipped easily into high society when they returned to
Puerto Rico. Their lives became a round of receptions for the
governor-general, the dignitary who represented Spain's domination of Puerto Rico prior to 1898.

Emilia, now sixty-five years old, relives a past filled with glittering jewels and Chopin waltzes. The house still contains furniture of
a past epoch "which knew luxury and refinement. A piano of rose
wood, . . . a Luis XV chair," and so forth ("mobiliario de una
época que conoció la suntuosidad y el refinamiento. Un piano de
palo de rosa, . . . una butaca Luis XV . . . " [I, 8]). The sisters, especially Emilia, find any intrusion of reality into these idealized
reminiscences intolerable. Emilia frequently closes the blinds and
lights lamps even when the sun is shining outdoors. Such gestures,
prescribed in the stage directions, underline the artificiality of these
lives that deny time and change.

The sisters' enclosure in the house stems from guilt. We learn in
the course of the play that the plain sisters (Inés considers herself
ugly; Emilia is lame, having fallen from a horse as a child) had

107

competed for the affections of an ensign destined to marry the beautiful Hortensia. As in the short story "Purification on Christ Street," Inés sabotages Hortensia's dream of marriage to the ensign by revealing that her fiancé has had a lover, a woman of inferior social station, and has fathered her child. Inés insists that she acts out of love for Hortensia; whether out of love or envy, she succeeds in destroying Hortensia's illusion. Hortensia then closes the doors of the house, and her sisters are shut in from life — penance for their sin of violating Hortensia's dream. To expiate their guilt, the sisters must preserve what is still beautiful for Hortensia — the jewels, the house, the memories.

Try as they may, the sisters cannot maintain their timeless existence; the certainty of change slips into the sisters' memories of nineteenth century Puerto Rican high society: relatives die, the estate is sold, the family jewels are dispersed. In the present, time intrudes into their world in the form of creditors. The two surviving sisters owe many years of taxes on the old house, and there is danger that the house will be sold at public auction. The Americans, in particular, would pay a great deal for such a house. The sisters must defend the status quo — their home — against American economic invasion. They recall their mother's attitude toward the coming of the Americans in 1898; Mama Eugenia viewed the Americans as barbarians because they bombarded churches, but more so because they bombarded the foundations of her world. In her lifetime, Hortensia reinforced the spirit of resistance by telling Emilia, "To resist is the password, Emilia. Resistance. In spite of hunger, time, and misery" ("Resistir es la consigna, Emilia. Resistir. A pesar del hambre, y el tiempo, y la miseria" [I, 37]). Inés, the more energetic sister, masterminds the actual resistance, feigning insanity when creditors knock at their door.

Refusing to surrender their home to those who would convert it to a luxury hotel, Emilia and Inés make a suicide pact. Marqués repeats from the short story "Purification on Christ Street" the symbolic stain on the wall, in the shape of two worlds connected by an isthmus. The sisters divorce themselves from the "continent" of time by breaking the connecting link. Wagnerian music, the unsold family jewels, the red and orange reflections of the fire keep the past intact. Emilia feels that the fire's reflection restores their beauty, that the act of resistance conquers time. They block out the sounds of the everyday world, the deafening horns, the creditors' knock at the door; they resist the growing intensity of natural light in Act II, which threatens the blue light of dream and fantasy. The sisters now seek through death to preserve their former world, symbolized at the end by the glittering diamond clasped in Inés' hand. Marqués universalizes the themes of guilt and expiation, as well as the concepts of resistance and dedication to an ideal, so frequent in his social drama. The Puerto Rican independence-seeker, taking on a collective guilt for his island's "ugliness" — its dependency on the United States — spends his life fighting for the freedom that will restore his island's beauty. The sisters' guilt over the destruction of beauty also sees them spending the rest of their lives in expiation for this crime. In the face of hunger, misery, and even death, they struggle to preserve the remnants of beauty in their world. The political threat is represented in the play by the American takeover of the house. Ironically, only the complete destruction of the house saves it from becoming a luxury hotel, which would house the laugh of vile, drunken tourists and the noisy digestion of bankers.

Written in the same year as *A Blue Child,* this drama reflects the artistic expertise of Marqués' peak dramatic period. Unlike *A Blue Child,* which frames a total act in flashback, *The Truncated Suns* continually shifts between past and present. Music makes the transition into the past. In the initial scene, Emilia hums a Chopin waltz as she is mopping the floor. She is suddenly removed from her prosaic existence, and with mop in hand, fantasizes a glittering reception where she talks to an imaginary young man. In each of the dead Hortensia's three appearances — at ages nineteen, thirty, and twenty-five, music initiates the dream scene. Music transports us from the red illumination of this life, into the blue light of dreams, and into the yellow light of eternity (Marqués retains the color symbolism of the truncated suns from the short story). The sisters' suicide is accompanied by dramatic, Wagnerian music. The song of the Walkyries is significant here, for it is played against the same purifying flames that devour Brunnhilde. The shift back to the present in the drama is usually effected by some auditory device from the real world, such as an automobile horn. A single auditory device may link the past and the present: in the scene recalling the death of papa Burkhart, one hears a knock at the door (the servants have carried the father's body home from the fields); this knock then moves to the present: creditors have come to tell the sisters that the house is no longer theirs. Marqués also uses lighting to signal these transitions. Purple light or blue dreamlike illumination transports us into fantasies of the past; normal light brings us back to the present.

The characters' continuing preoccupation with time and death also links past with present. Emilia reflects this preoccupation both in her dialogue with the young gentleman in the imagined "past" (where she apprises him of the sale of family jewels and the loss of the estate) and in her heroic pronouncement of the "present" that she would prefer death to loss of the house. Her statement is followed by a fantasy sequence, in which Hortensia relives the death of their mother and other relatives and also the spiritual "death" brought by the American invasion of Puerto Rico. We also learn that the sisters' jealousy has caused yet another kind of destruction. The focus shifts once again to the present, as the tasteless coffin sent for Hortensia by public welfare arrives at the house. In Act II, the three sisters relive the death of their father against the background of a funeral march. The theme of death culminates in the dramatic present, with the immolation of the two surviving sisters.

One excellent scene that links past with present is the memory of the father's death. Inés narrates, while Emilia and Hortensia act out the events. Time for the sisters is fused here. Inés remains in the present with her narration, while Hortensia and Emilia dramatize the past.

Marqués choreographs the dramatic action with explicit stage directions, which often replace dialogue with pantomime. In one scene Emilia descends the stairs carrying Hortensia's wedding dress in her hands — the dress that Hortensia will now wear in death. Inés orders Emilia to put the dress in Hortensia's room; Marqués specifies silent gestures:

Emilia opens the door and exits. Inés goes slowly to the back of the stage. She approaches one of the closed doors. She rests her forehead upon the door, then extends her arms as if she wanted to embrace the door and sobs. . . .

Emilia enters from the right, closing the door behind her. She sees Inés in the background and becomes confused. She takes some indecisive steps. Finally she slips secretly toward the staircase. But instead of ascending, she remains on the first step. Slowly she slips to the floor without taking her eyes off Inés. She sits curled up into a ball, and remains there, silent as a frightened child, biting a nail, observing Inés across the bannisters. Inés has been calming herself, turns around, approaches the piano and rests on it. She wipes her eyes with her finger tips.

(Emilia abre la puerta y sale de escena. Inés va lentamente al fondo. Se acerca a una de las puertas cerradas. Apoya la frente sobre la puerta, luego extiende los brazos como si quisiera abrazarse a la puerta, y solloza. . . . Entra Emilia por la derecha, cerrando la puerta tras de sí. Ve a Inés en el fondo y se desconcierta. Da unos pasos indecisos. Al fin se desliza sigilosamente hasta la escalera. Pero en vez de subir, se queda en el primer escalón. Lentamente se va escurriendo hasta el piso sin dejar de mirar a Inés. Se sienta hecha un ovillo en el escalón y se queda allí quieta, como un niño asustado, mordiéndose una uña, observando a Inés a través de los balaustres de la escalera. Inés se ha ido calmando, se vuelve, se acerca al piano y se apoya en él. Se limpia los ojos con las yemas de los dedos [II, 47–48].)

These gestures poignantly suggest what might have been — Hortensia's marriage to the ensign. The emblem of the wedding dress makes concrete the sisters' sorrow and guilt for their part in Hortensia's "death."

The Truncated Suns powerfully portrays individuals ruled by an obsession — the preservation of recollected beauty. The villain of the drama is time, which is dedicated to the destruction of this ideal. Set in Puerto Rico, the play has distinct political innuendos and comments on the American invasion of Puerto Rico in 1898 — but, decidedly, the political issue is not dominant. In the next play analyzed, Marqués again presents political issues, but also becomes concerned with universal dilemmas of the modern world.

II   Carnaval afuera, carnaval adentro (Carnival Outside, Carnival Inside)

Written in the same year as *The House Without a Clock*, *Carnival Outside, Carnival Inside* continues Marqués commentary on the absurdity of modern Puerto Rican society. Puerto Rico's acceptance of foreign domination is mirrored in the microcosm of one family — Mary, her husband Willie, and their daughter Rosita. They welcome into their home foreigners: the Cuban countess and her North American administrator, George, who wish to buy the island; and Pito Jilguera (modeled after José Figueres Ferrer, former president of Costa Rica), whose historic collaboration with North America becomes a prototype for the Puerto Rican sellout to the United States. Marqués pits these characters against those who represent Puerto Rican indigenous elements: the grandmother Doña Rosa, Aunt Matilde, and the *Vegigantes* (masked carnival celebrators) who represent the Spanish, Indian, and African elements of Puerto Rico.

At the same time, *Carnival Outside, Carnival Inside* portrays the universal problems of modern society. The characters are emblematic of such phenomena as mechanization, materialism, hypocrisy, and paucity of communication. The maid Felicita speaks and acts like a locomotive: "Tut-tut, tut-tut, tut-tut-tut."[2] Hyperbole emphasizes Mary's materialism: she owns one hundred pairs of shoes, one hundred dresses, one hundred jewels, a cottage that she will soon exchange for an estate on Dorado Beach, and a Mercedes Benz that will soon give way to a Rolls Royce.

The countess' materialism is revealed when she laments her exile from her beloved island:

I was alone in New York. Alone, suffering the unspoken anguish of the exiled. Lost in that horrible whirlpool. I would go from my *suite* in the Waldorf Astoria to my apartment on Fifth Avenue. And when the pain of exile would lacerate my heart, I would leave for my villa in Miami or fly to my *chateau* on the Côte d'Azur and end up, as always, becoming bored in my *chalet* in the Swiss Alps. That's all that was left.
GEORGE: And the eight million in stock.

(Estaba yo sola en New York. Sola, sufriendo la indecible angustia del expatriado. Perdida en aquella horrible vorágine. Iba yo de mi *suite* del Waldorf Astoria a mi apartamiento de la Quinta Avenida. Y cuando el dolor del exilio laceraba mi corazón, partía hacia mi villa en Miami o volaba a mi *chateau* de la Costa Azul para concluir, como siempre, aburriéndome en mi *chalet* de los Alpes suizos. Sólo eso me quedaba . . . .
GEORGE. — Y los ocho millones en acciones [II, 62].)

The countess is also the model of hypocrisy: she claims to love the Negroes she employed in Cuba but they were paid no wages. When she sees the Negro maid Felicita, the "unbiased" countess faints — an action that Pito comically calls antidemocratic.

The characters' interactions reflect the lack of communication that was so telling in *The House Without a Clock*. Recalling how she learned that Puerto Rico was "for sale," the countess explains that she immediately called her manager George:

GEORGE: Pardon me, Countess. It was I who called you.
COUNTESS: But you were in the bathroom, George! I remember well.
GEORGE: I had on my bathrobe, but I was *not* in the bathroom.

. . . .

COUNTESS: It was tea time on the terrace.
GEORGE: We were eating breakfast. I remember that we were drinking coffee in the garden.
COUNTESS: The tea had gotten cold. How you quarreled, George!
GEORGE: Because the coffee was very strong. You know, Countess, that it irritates my nerves.
MARY: And the island?
COUNTESS: What island?
WILLIE: The one in the advertisement.
GEORGE: What advertisement?
PITO: We were talking about coffee.
RASPUTO [nephew of the Countess]: I detest coffee. It's vile.
PITO: Nonsense. We all know that the price of coffee has dropped. It is a hemispheric problem.

(GEORGE. — Perdona, Condesa. Fui yo quien te llamó a ti.
CONDESA. — ¡Pero estabas en el baño, George! Lo recuerdo perfectamente.
GEORGE. — Tenía puesta la bata de baño, pero *no* estaba en el baño.
. . . .
CONDESA. — Era la hora del té en la terraza.
GEORGE. — Nos desayunábamos. Recuerdo que tomábamos café en el jardín.
CONDESA. — El té se había enfriado. ¡Cómo peleaste, George!
GEORGE. — Porque el café era muy fuerte. Sabes, Condesa, que me irrita los nervios.
MARY. — ¿Y la isla?
CONDESA. — ¿Qué isla?
WILLIE. — La del anuncio.
GEORGE. — ¿Qué anuncio?
PITO. — Hablábamos del café.
RASPUTO. — Detesto el café. Es vulgar.
PITO. — Tonterías. Todos sabemos que el precio del café ha bajado. Es un problem hemisférico [II, 72].)

Disjointed dialogue recurs when the countess denounces monopoly as unjust, and Willie rejoins that monopoly is an interesting game. This initiates a ridiculous discussion of preferences for Chinese checkers, chess, and other games.

Marqués has no intention of being subtle in this work. His characters bombard the audience with a stacatto enumeration of social ills. The artist Angel delivers the following diatribe:

standardization   (estandarización

transculturation	transculturación
gangsterization	gangsterización
conscription	conscripción
militarization	militarización
sterilization	esterilización
. . . . . .	. . . . . .
drug addiction	droga-adicción
exploitation	explotación
. . . . . .	. . . . . .
radio activation	radiativación
contamination	contaminación
Circumcision!	Circuncisión!
And, of course...	Y, desde luego...
assimilation.	asimilación [I, 41–42].)

Social ills are named over and over again, as characters mention censorship, the Vietnam war, racial intolerance, narcotics, mechanization, capital punishment, overpopulation, overemphasis on science, overextended credit, pollution, and so forth. They also specify the maladies peculiar to Puerto Rico: urbanization, the presence of elements in the population (Yankees, Cubans, various religious denominations) that support the status quo, imprisonment of nationalists, absenteeism, North American naval bases in the Caribbean, industrialization, political dependency. The expressionistic, rapid fire listing of these problems has a cumulative effect, impressing upon the audience their gravity and the fear that spiritual or cultural values cannot survive these overwhelming ills.

And, in fact, this society as it is depicted on stage does lack the spiritual elements — art, love, liberty — that for Marqués are of the utmost importance. Only the artist Angel has internalized these values, and in the course of the play, he is able to show Rosita, the daughter of the typically "establishment" family, the merits of his outlook. She rebels against her family's plans to marry her off to "Mack" (a name that stands for the establishment). Rosita's love for Angel allows her to accept his world, and with him she must suffer the vengeance of a society that cannot tolerate the values so "prejudicial" to Mack. Angel is placed on trial, and Doña Rosa defends him, prompted by Aunt Matilde. Willie and the Countess, dressed in the attire of medieval inquisitors, serve as judges, and George is the prosecuting attorney. Rasputo represents the church, and Pito, the government; both sanction this monkey trial and the eventual condemnation and torture of Angel.

The torture of Angel is only relieved when Rosita agrees to sacrifice herself to society's demand for retribution. She sacrifices herself so that the spiritual may survive. She gives Angel the freedom he needs to save his world. Angel has triumphed within the house; the farce has ended. Yet he must now face the larger farce — the carnival — outside the door. The audience is left to conjecture as to Angel's ultimate fate.

Carnival Outside, Carnival Inside is a farce — a genre that dates back to Aristophanes, the Roman comedy, and the Italian *commedia dell'arte*. Aunt Matilde directs the farce, as if she were the ringleader in a circus. The play begins with a crack of a whip, circus music, and Aunt Matilde's call for Curtain! Lights! Actors on stage! The actors are conscious participants in the farce. When Rosa confuses her cue, Aunt Matilde acts as prompter. She reprimands the actors if they depart from the text. The script is a metaphor for the dictates of modern society, from which the actors cannot deviate. The text is altered only momentarily, when Marqués' own elusive ideals are dramatized by Angel and Rosita.

The disharmony of this world is echoed in the play's discordant tones: strident music, drum rolls, bugles, automobile horns. Sounds are only muted and made harmonious as we approach the world of the spirit; violins play as Angel kisses Rosita. The use of pantomime and masks stresses the artificiality of human interaction in this world. Angel unmasks Rosita when he kisses her, signifying her entrance into a more natural realm.

As in other plays, transitions between scenes or acts are especially good. At the outset, the theater is dark and one hears the sounds of the world outside the house — of progress (automobile horns) and of a past epoch (the trotting of a horse). One hears voices in Spanish and English that express irritation at the horse, which is creating a traffic jam. In the mounting tension, North Americans and Cubans criticize Puerto Ricans. This outside world mirrors what will be dramatized inside the house: the same carnival of progress, of North Americans and Cubans who do not appreciate Puerto Rico, the intense division among human beings. The cracking of the whip over the horse provides an excellent transition to the cracking of Aunt Matilde's whip, as she begins to direct the farce within the house.

One innovative transition is that between Acts I and II. At the end of Act I, Willie and Mary are expecting guests, but suddenly find themselves faced with the presence of the "horrible" *vegi-*

gantes, from whom they try to escape. Act II finds a re-do of the ending of Act I, this time with the arrival of the countess, George, Rasputo, and Pito Jilguera. In the Strindberg tradition of ignoring time and space, Marqués portrays the fear of the indigenous and the acceptance of foreign elements in Puerto Rico.

As in some of his earlier plays, Marqués' social message at times becomes overbearing, as in the heavyhanded characterization of George — a magical reproducer of money, maker of wars, fomenter of hatred, friend of the atom, and sworn enemy of subversion, a person authorized to rob, plunder, bribe, blackmail, defraud, and to exploit. The play also tends at times to be excessively narrow in scope and therefore is not always intelligible to a foreign audience. For example, Rasputo and George at one point discuss the Christian Democrats — alluding to the New Catholic Action party registered in 1960, criticized by Marqués in his essay "The Docile Puerto Rican."[3]

Carnival Outside, Carnival Inside is a play that seems to give equal billing to political issues and problems of modern society. Puerto Rico is a microcosm for its own particular difficulties, as well as for those of the modern epoch. In the next play, Marqués leaves the Puerto Rican scene and locates his characters in an "apartment" cut off from the rest of the world. The characters, though, reflect social ills common to all of Latin America, as well as the problems of modern society.

III   El apartamiento (The Apartment)

In the existential drama *The Apartment* (1964), Marqués relates the degradation of modern man[4] to his enclosure in a world of technology and specialization, where his creative powers are sacrificed to science and his spiritual needs are ignored. Like Rodó and Mallea, Marqués was acutely concerned with the loss of creativity throughout Latin America, and he stated that *The Apartment* could be set in any part of the Americas. He locates his characters in an apartment, shut off from the outside world.[5] In its confines, a couple, Carola and Elpidio, are provided with every material comfort. Carola need not clean house, for the air in the apartment is scientifically filtered, preventing dust from settling on the furniture. Nor does Carola have to cook; meals arrive promptly and regularly through a dumbwaiter, which also disposes of soiled clothes. Wearing apparel is always ironed, and used kitchen utensils are incinerated and replaced. The couple's existence is controlled by "Them" (*ellos*) — the inspectors Landrilo and Cuprila — who make sure that Carola and Elpidio carry out their specialized tasks: Carola must measure a blue ribbon and Elpidio must assemble a puzzle in the form of a man. Marqués draws on Samuel Beckett's *Waiting for Godot,* in which the characters' pastimes are designed to prevent thought. As in George Orwell's *1984,* [6] the characters' minds are programmed by the censored mass media. Carola and Elpidio must watch prescribed television programs: one for men featuring puzzle assembly technique and one for women with instructions for measuring blue ribbon. To maintain their comfortable existence in the apartment, they must also conform to orders: the erasure of memory, the negation of will and creative power.

Marqués draws heavily on Sartre's *No Exit,* Harold Pinter's *The Dumb Waiter,* and Ionesco's *Amédée, or How to Get Rid of It* in his conception of the apartment itself. There are no windows, and the only door leads to an endless corridor. [7] The elevator leads nowhere, and does not even provide the sensation of movement. As in *The House Without a Clock,* time is at a standstill for the inhabitants of the stage world. Night and day as sequential predictable phenomena do not exist for the couple. Carola tells us, "One turns off the light and it is nighttime. One turns on the light and it is daytime" ("Se apaga la luz y es noche. Se enciende la luz, y es día" [II, 85]). Their conversations make arbitrary tense shifts — present, past, and future are interchangeable in a context where present is past and future. The desire to escape, perhaps a once fervent wish, has been reduced to a mechanical act — looking for a door at the end of an elevator "ride." Having gone through this routine for years, Carola and Elpidio know full well that there is no exit.

In Marqués' terms, the only exit, the only liberation, is through rejection of this passive and alienated life and through active formulation and pursuit of ideals. This process involves acceptance of one's own individual and cultural identity. For Marqués' characters Elpidio and Carola, confrontation with their own past ideals and cultural roots takes the form of dealing with three troubling intruders: a young man called Lucío; a woman, Terra; and the Indian, Tlo. In the case of Lucío and Terra, Marqués does not use flashback, but instead creates a kind of double for each character to remind them of their youth and lost ideals. The play focuses on the couple's ambivalence toward this intrusion into their humdrum existence.

Through Lucío, we learn of Elpidio's past: his composition of the Symphony of the Stars; his appreciation of nature, culture, roots. We also learn how he sacrificed himself for the sake of Lucío, who represents ideals — ideals later betrayed for money. Terra reminds Carola of her feats as poetess of America, of her love for mankind, but also of the jealousy that caused her to shun her lover Orestes (symbol of sacrifice, action, ideals)[8] and Terra (symbol of the land), believing them to be untrue to her. Elpidio and Carola are captivated by the poetic reverie of this past life; but they ultimately reject the fantasy and return to their sterile existence. In this way, Marqués informs us that the spiritual element cannot survive. Terra and Lucío, representing ideals, have no independent existence. They live only within individuals, and if rejected by them, they fade away or conform to the lives that the individuals choose: Terra moves symbolically to Carola's table and begins to measure the ribbon. Lucío takes up Elpidio's task of assembling the puzzle. A violet light illuminates them both, suggesting nobility. Although they stubbornly reaffirm the reality that Carola and Elpidio want to deny — that there lived a famous poetess and composer — their mission is ultimately unsuccessful. At the end, the inspectors carry the lifeless bodies of Terra and Lucío onto the stage.

Tlo, however, cannot be done away with so readily. The Indian, who represents Latin American cultural roots, is held captive by the inspectors, who order Carola and Elpidio to kill him. Tlo tells Carola and Elpidio that for years he has wanted to destroy the lifeless existence of the apartment. Carola and Elpidio cannot kill the man who personifies their culture. Carola believes that the Indian will someday destroy their hermetic existence. Instead of killing him with a knife, she cuts the cords that bind the Indian's hands and gives him the knife. She liberates and fortifies her culture and calls this her duty. In the denouement, the armed Indian Tlo disappears to carry out his mission of destroying mediocrity and restoring culture. The curtain falls as Carola goes to answer the doorbell. Elpidio says that the open door may bring death — perhaps admitting the inspectors who will kill them for having freed the Indian. Carola hopes the open door will lead to liberation — the victorious return of the Indian. Marqués leaves the outcome to the audience's imagination.

The play suffers from rhetoric (for example, that of the Indian figure Tlo); yet Marqués' social ideas are also presented in literary and theatrical imagery. Stage effects contrast man's deadened existence with the vital force of ideals. Terra and Lucío's normal appearance contrasts with the funereal makeup worn by Carola and Elpidio. The husband and wife converse in laconic, dry dialogue — deadened by their boredom. This contrasts with the poetic, profuse speech of Lucío:

You have to go to the heart of your land, know the peasant, ascend the mountain, travel through the small coastal villages, and the old colonial towns. You have to look for your roots before attempting to elevate yourself to the regions of creation.

(Tienes que ir a la entraña de tu tierra, conocer al campesino, ascender a la montaña, recorrer las pequeñas aldeas costaneras, y los viejos pueblos coloniales. Tienes que buscar la raíz de lo tuyo antes de intentar elevarte a las regiones de la creación [I, 55].)

Marqués again uses blue light to illuminate images of the ideal. When for one brief moment, Elpidio and Carola each are swayed by these ideals, the blue light is cast over them. When the spell is broken, normal illumination returns. The Indian is also presented under a blue light; in contrast, Cuprila and Landrilo make their initial appearance under red illumination.

As in other plays, music provides contrast. Strident music signifying man's sterile existence contrasts with the music of the flute or with an Indian melody. Cuprila and Landrilo enter to the tune of strident, discordant music. When Tlo is made captive, the same strains signify the triumph of mediocrity. Carola's rejection of ideals signals an abrupt end to the Indian music that accompanied her dialogue, and this marks the eradication of the spiritual.

Simple contrast is the basic technique here, but the drama also contains subtle shadings. The seemingly pessimistic destruction of ideals and creativity is counterbalanced by Carola's acceptance and defense of her culture. And this acceptance, for Marqués, will prevent future destruction of Lucío and Terra. As Lucío states, acceptance of one's culture elevates man to the regions of creation. Marqués hopes to instill this positive message in his audience and in his fellow Latin Americans.

The Apartment contains a back and forth movement of the characters toward this solution. The denouement is also reached through recognition of inner necessities, more so than outward influence. Man's repressed needs ultimately surge forth and take over his character, leaving him no choice but to heed and satisfy them by pursuing spiritual goals.

In the three dramas analyzed in this chapter, Marqués depicts universal themes — the ravages of time, the preservation of ideals, and the social problems of modern society. Insurmountable ideals conquer time in *The Truncated Suns* and fortify man for the struggle against social ills in *Carnival Outside, Carnival Inside* and *The Apartment*. Puerto Rico's problems are also interspersed in these works; and in *The Apartment,* Marqués' social mission sees him depicting Puerto Rico's cultural loss as a problem common to all of Latin America. Marqués reached a stylistic peak in *The Truncated Suns*. *Carnival Outside, Carnival Inside* is a weaker play, which relies too heavily on political rhetoric; but *The Apartment,* despite the rhetoric of the Indian figure Tlo, returns to the vivid portrayal of social ills in dramatic imagery. The simplicity of the staging in *The Apartment* recalls Marqués' early work and prepares the way for his ultimate drama.

CHAPTER 9

Biblical Drama

I N his last three plays, the dramatist uses biblical themes to portray the foibles of twentieth century man, and to demonstrate
the perpetuation of human weakness. He cites Ecclesiastes, 1,9
"What has been, will always be; / what has been done, will be done
in the future; / there is nothing new under the sun." ("Lo que fue,
siempre será; / lo que se hizo, lo mismo se hará; / nada hay de
nuevo bajo el sol").[1] In these works Marqués takes liberties with
biblical accounts and with history in order to communicate his own
vision of the human condition.[2]

I   Sacrificio en el Monte Moriah (Sacrifice on Mount Moriah)

In *Sacrifice on Mount Moriah* (1969), set in fourteen scenes,
Marqués takes us back four thousand years, to the society of the
patriarch Abraham, his wife Sarah, and their son Isaac, where we
witness the characters' familial and social problems. Abraham is
both a colonizer (of Chanaan) and a colonial subject of Egypt. His
god is the warring and fanatical Yahvé, who permits no opposition.
Sarah is therefore not allowed to worship her god, Nannar; nor
may the Chanaanites adore their god Baal. For this god, the
patriarch is even willing to sacrifice his son — Isaac — on Mount
Moriah. It is only through Sarah's intervention that Isaac is saved.
Conscious that Abraham will only heed divine intervention, she
appears before her husband disguised as an angel. After this Isaac
resists Abraham's world. On his eighteenth birthday, Isaac bids his
family farewell, rejecting the god Yahvé who would permit a father
to sacrifice his son. He prefers, in contrast, a god of love and
peace, of kindness and liberty, who would never demand ritual
sacrifice. Sarah supports Isaac's departure and, in the denouement,
kills Abraham, thereby freeing the entire nation from subjugation
to Yahvé.

Marqués tells us that the events portrayed in this drama may be projected to today's world,[3] and especially to Puerto Rico. Some of the historic parallels drawn by Marqués are quite obvious. For example, when Chanaan becomes a target of imperialistic invasion, Abraham abandons his adopted land and flees to Egypt, where he asks the pharaoh's protection. He asks to be associated with the pharaoh, who responds by questioning the word "associated." Abraham hastens to clarify his meaning — "subordinated." The price of association is the favors of Abraham's wife, in return for which Abraham receives not only protection, but also riches. The situation clearly parallels Puerto Rico's association with the United States, and the audience is reminded of how Luis Muñoz Marín refused to defend the liberty of his land, courting United States protection for the sake of material benefits and ultimately selling out Puerto Rico to the interests of the stronger power. In this same scene, the Egyptian pharaoh is reminded by his prime minister that Chanaan has strategic value; Egypt's commercial caravans, traveling to the kingdoms of Mesopotamia, must pass through Chanaan. Marqués draws a parallel with Puerto Rico's historical strategic value as a military base for foreign countries. In another scene, Sarah calls Abraham docile, because he is subservient to Yahvé. Marqués dramatizes here the docility of the Puerto Rican as well, who has blind faith in the North American "deity" and accepts the god's imposition of alien values on his land.

Perhaps a more subtle allegory is seen in Sarah's actions. The woman mocks her husband's fanatical adherence to a warring god by tricking him. When Yahvé promises Abraham descendants, Sarah fulfills the prophecies of this god. She arranges for the servant Agar to cohabit with Abraham, but only she and Agar know that the child, Ismael, was fathered not by the aging Abraham, but by a young Jewish shepherd. Sixteen years later Sarah again deceives Abraham, when she bears a son, Isaac, who is fathered by Ismael. Motivated by ambition, she reveals that Ismael is not Abraham's son. She casts Agar and Ismael from her house and plays on Abraham's unquestioning faith by assuring him that Isaac is his legal son, conceived by a miracle from God.

This complex family situation holds a political message for Marqués' audience. Addressing Puerto Ricans who regard North America as a kind of deity, Marqués hopes to demystify the power structure. He debunks superstitious worship of unworthy gods and shows how the promises of an "omnipotent" deity are in fact ful-

filled by human machinations. By dramatizing the birth of Isaac —
a human scheme that Abraham believes to be a divine miracle —
Marqués calls on the Puerto Rican who accepts the Northern
"miracle" on his island to look beyond the myth.
Marqués also uses this play as a vehicle to criticize the Vietnam
War. He draws a parallel between Abraham's submission to the
warring god Yahvé and the Puerto Rican's submission to the mili-
tant United States in Vietnam. He also parallels Isaac's rejection of
Yahvé and Marqués' own son Raúl's refusal to serve in the United
States forces in Vietnam. In the dedication to the drama, the author
supports his son's rebellion and states that, unlike Abraham, he
cannot contemplate sacrifice of his son to the whims of the Northern "deity":

To Raúl, my first-born, who has refused, following the dictates of his conscience, to enter the army under the law of obligatory military service, and
whom I would never be prepared to sacrifice on the altars of any bloody
and warring being, I dedicate, with admiration as a Puerto Rican and with
a father's love and pride, *Sacrificio en el Monte Moriah*.

(A él, Raúl, mi primogénito, quien ha rehusado, siguiendo los dictados de
su conciencia, ingresar en el ejército mediante la ley de Servicio Militar
Obligatorio y a quien yo jamás estaría dispuesto a sacrificar en aras de ningún ente sanguinario y belicista, dedico, con admiración de puertorriqueño y entrañable amor y orgullo de padre, *Sacrificio en el Monte
Moriah* [p. 47].)

Both Isaac and Raúl are, for Marqués, liberated men. Yet his
choice of Isaac as a rebel is puzzling, for in the Bible, Isaac seems
unable to avoid his father's mistakes: Abraham's prostitution of
Sarah repeats itself in Isaac, who for the sake of wealth attempts to
submit his wife Rebecca to Abimelech,[4] king of the Philistines. It
seems strange that Marqués chose as his symbol of liberalism a man
destined to fall. Perhaps Marqués is saying that the fall of a would-
be liberator is inevitable in any age? That ideals are elusive in the
face of the barriers presented by human nature? Isaac's "fall" may
be suggested in the finale of the play, when the chorus, triumphant
at the beginning of the drama, becomes plaintive and woeful in the
denouement. The sentinel who at the outset announces the dawn, in
the denouement predicts a future filled with horror.
Isaac manages to free himself from Abraham's values, but he
still represents a nation built on false bases, since he is not really

Abraham's son. We recall the biblical passage quoted in *Death Shall Not Enter the Palace,* telling us that a nation built on false bases cannot stand.

Notwithstanding the ambiguity of Marqués' message, the play is noteworthy for its stylistic innovations. At the outset, Sarah recollects incidents that lead to the dramatic present. Flashback stagings of these events are then scattered throughout the drama. Marqués refines the flashback technique by calling for either a revolving stage or a stage composed of several platforms that can be illuminated at different times. Marqués also makes ingenious use of lighting in this drama. The effect is almost cinematographic when lighting gives the impression of closeups. During the sacrifice scene, the theater is darkened, with a single beam of white light cast on Abraham's hand, which clasps the knife. Sarah appears as an angel under a blue light, and after she prevents the sacrifice, the closeup of Abraham's hand gradually fades out. The "closeup" is again utilized in the supper scene, before Isaac's departure. The focus on the faces of Isaac and Abraham as father is about to strike son emphasizes their alienation. When Isaac offers the knife, suggesting caustically that his father attempt to sacrifice him once again, the focus shifts to Isaac's hand. At another moment, after Sarah kills Abraham, the spotlight falls on the enormous sacrificial knife, stained with fresh blood. The "closeup" technique provides continuity by tracing the role of the knife from attempted oblation for superstitious reasons to actual sacrifice for national goals.

An innovative visual element is also utilized in the supper scene: when Abraham cannot carve the roasted lamb, because he is reminded of the attempted offering on Mount Moriah, Marqués emphasizes the patriarch's recall of this event by introducing in the background a silhouette scene of the attempted sacrifice.

As in other dramas, Marqués is adept at integrating visual and auditory effects. In the first scene, the stage is illuminated by a red light; one hears the voice of a prophet who denounces those who seek help from others instead of looking to their own hearts. The audience also listens to the choral lament and the voice of Sarah telling Abraham he will die. The sacrificial knife that will play such an important role appears in closeup, held by an unseen hand. The audience is then witness to a kind of psychedelic ballet in the tradition of Artaud; knives, swords, and daggers appear in chaotic fashion on different levels and in different positions; these weapons move in attack patterns with slow, rhythmic movement.

A similar combination of devices suggests the splendor of the pharaoh's court — the glitter of gold and elegant clothes, music and dance, and the smell of incense create an atmosphere that appeals to the senses.

Several scenes are noted for the excellent display of emotions: scene *i,* for the portrayal of the conjugal conflict between Abraham and Sarah; scene *iii,* for the presentation of Isaac's suspicions and fears prior to the attempted sacrifice on Mount Moriah. Symbolism is paramount in the scene depicting Sarah's seduction of Ismael: the release of a male goat paves the way for the release of Ismael's sexual desires when faced with Sarah's sensuality.

In his last two dramas, Marqués uses more simplified staging. But he continues the theme of Ecclesiastes and utilizes biblical history as commentary on social and political conditions in Puerto Rico.

II David y Jonatán (David and Jonathan)

Marqués dramatizes the short-lived dominance of Isaac's doctrine of peace, kindness, and love in his next two dramas. *David and Jonathan* and *Titus and Bernice* (1970) are grouped together in a single volume subtitled *Dos dramas de amor, poder y desamor (Two Dramas of Love, Power, and Hate).* The subtitle capsulizes the theme of the two works: craving power, men invariably reject the humanitarian values of love and tolerance. This pattern holds for every male protagonist of both plays, creating a very pessimistic vision of human nature. In order to communicate his personal view, Marqués again takes liberties with historical and scriptural accounts.

In *David and Jonathan,* Marqués moves from the days of the Patriarch Abraham (1900 B.C.) to the period of 1000 B.C., when the Jewish nation was ruled by priest-judges and was evolving toward monarchy. The character most obsessed with power in this play is the priest-judge Samuel, who is viewed as the spokesman for the sovereign — God. When his people clamor for a human monarch to protect them against the Philistines,[5] Samuel anoints the warrior-shepherd Saul as king, shrewdly appeasing the nation's fear. In response to an acolyte's concern at the priest-judge's diminished power, Samuel first feigns humility before the will of God, but later reveals his true intent: "behind every throne there will always be a priest, who will also be judge" ("...detrás del

trono siempre habrá un sacerdote, que también será juez'' [*iii*, 28]).
The people will have their king, so long as Saul serves Samuel's
purposes.

Samuel guarantees his power behind the throne by creating
power rivalries between David and Saul and between David and
Saul's son Jonathan. The outcome is tragic: pursued by David and
Samuel, who have allied themselves with the Philistines, Saul commits suicide, and Jonathan dies at David's hands. Samuel has
manipulated political dissent in order to control the throne and has
thereby put his nation through a terrible ordeal.

Love is short-lived in this drama. Saul's momentary wish to exchange power for the greater gift of love (he removes the crown
that has weighed on him so heavily and lets it drop to the floor) succumbs to a power struggle when David becomes a rival to the
throne. The love between Jonathan and David is also undermined
by ambition. After his father's death, Jonathan fights against
David because he believes that David has betrayed their love:
''Saul's blood will fall upon your head. And on your people,
generation after generation. You renounced love, when love was
the only possible salvation'' (''la sangre de Saúl caerá sobre tu
cabeza. Y sobre todos los tuyos, generación tras generación. Pues
renegaste del amor, cuando era el amor la salvación única, la
posible'' [*x*, 53]).

Jonathan has understood the power of hatred even before the
denouement, for he has said, ''hatred stalks us, surrounds us. . . .
It is a world of hatred and blood, where there is no room for love''
(''el odio nos acecha, nos rodea. . . . Es un mundo de odio y sangre,
donde no cabe el amor'' [*ix*, 50]). And the dying Jonathan finalizes
this concept with the words: ''Love . . . dies'' (''El amor . . .
muere'' [*x*, 54]).

In the denouement, David laments his foul deeds, but is fortified
by the cold reason of Samuel, who tells him that he did what had to
be done in order to become king. Marqués makes it clear that
Samuel will retain actual power. In the end, hatred completely
dominates Samuel, Saul's potential love is thwarted, and the real
love between David and Jonathan is destroyed. Just as Jonathan's
nudity disquiets his sister Mikol and David (scene *vii*), Marqués'
exposed characters make the audience uncomfortable by dramatizing human weakness.

Like *Sacrifice on Mount Moriah, David and Jonathan* bears a
political relationship to modern-day Puerto Rico. The power strug-

gle recalls the figure of Luis Muñoz Marín, who was thought to have sacrificed his nation's independence to the pursuit of power. Samuel's furtive manipulation of national figureheads suggests the manipulation of the Puerto Rican government by the United States during the era of American governors in Puerto Rico prior to 1947, as well as after the establishment of the commonwealth. Samuel sometimes appears as a somber figure, smiling in the background, or as a figure who seems to surge up from the bowels of the earth. The allegory is more subtle than that of *Sacrifice*. Also, Marqués does not weaken the allegory, as he did in *Sacrifice*, by attempting to express too broad a political platform in a single drama.

David and Jonathan is divided into ten scenes. The chronological movement is disrupted only once; scene *v* is set two days before scene *iv*. The drama is surprisingly stark, with relatively simple dialogue, stage setting, and special effects. Stage directions are quite brief, which is uncharacteristic for Marqués. The only symbolic stage device is Saul's movable throne: as it recedes into the background, it dramatizes the king's growing alienation from family and friends. Scenes *i* and *v* are set behind a gauze curtain, which creates the illusion of distance and stylizes the action. As in his earlier work, Marqués uses music to make mood shifts: martial strains in the first scene dramatize the nation's fear of the Philistines. In scene *iii,* a sheep horn warns of the enemy's attack. David's citara, (a stringed instrument used in antiquity), heard in scene *iv* when Samuel brings David to court, suggests the onset of peace and harmony, to soothe Saul's nerves. But David, already anointed as future king by Samuel, will ultimately bring discord. The conflict between Jonathan and David in scene *ix* is accompanied by battle sounds and then bucolic music — war and peace. But ultimately, war triumphs and Jonathan dies.

Marqués intended for *David and Jonathan* to be staged together with *Titus and Bernice,* which reinforces his cynical vision of man as a political creature.

III Tito y Berenice (Titus and Bernice)

Set in the Roman Empire in 70–81 A.D., *Titus and Bernice* again shows love thwarted by the pursuit of power. Bernice, princess of the state of Israel, is in love with Titus, future sovereign of the Roman Empire. She must suffer separation from her lover when he becomes emperor and must carry out governmental duties in

Rome. In his new capacity, he is not allowed to marry a foreigner. But separated from his love, Titus is unable to perform his duties as ruler. The president of the senate describes Titus' dissipation, recalling that the new emperor had once been a general who had won glory: "But as emperor, you have neglected the government; you have dedicated yourself more to pleasure than to duty; you serve more your personal appetites than the well-being of the empire" (Pero como emperador has descuidado las cosas de gobierno; te has dedicado más al placer que al deber; sirves más a tus apetitos personales que al bienestar del imperio" [*vii,* 84]).

Unlike the ruler Don José, who thwarts Puerto Rico's well-being for personal ambitions, in *Titus and Bernice,* Titus makes a moral comeback. The eruption of the volcano in Pompeii, which vents nature's fury against those who have betrayed their own nature as well as their nation, prompts his reform: "the external disaster made me turn my eyes to the internal disaster, to my own ruin. Since then, . . . I have been . . . a just and equitable ruler . . ." ("el desastre exterior me hizo volver los ojos al desastre interior, al mío propio. Desde entonces, . . . he sido . . . un gobernante justo y equitativo, . . ." [*viii,* 89]).

Titus becomes responsive to Rome, and not to his weaknesses — to the national welfare, and not to personal interest. Also, he is now prepared to renounce his throne for the sake of the love he left behind. The Roman Senate considers the possible dangers that could be provoked by the renunciation of the popular sovereign — insurrection, and perhaps civil war — and sanctions his marriage to Bernice. But the ravages of time have withered Bernice, and Titus cannot accept her flaws. He returns to Rome alone. Marqués uses sound effects to recall his coronation — the voices of the populace hailing Titus as Caesar — which marked his ascent to power. Once again, ambition has conquered love.

As in the preceding drama, the incidents portrayed parallel Puerto Rican historical events. Just as Abraham fled from Chanaan, besieged by invaders, so too King Herod flees from Jerusalem when the city is invaded by Roman forces. Abraham's prostitution of Sarah for the sake of protection is repeated in King Herod, who sends his daughter Bernice to Titus to buy Roman protection with her favors. Once again, Marqués draws a parallel with modern Puerto Rico, which even after Luis Muñoz Marín's tenure as governor, in his eyes continued to sell itself for the sake of foreign protection.

The love between Bernice and Titus contains a subtle political commentary. Bernice symbolizes Judea or Israel, conquered by Titus' Roman forces. The colony is loved at first sight by the colonizer. Titus initially sees Bernice as an equal: "Why not speak in terms of two human beings, what does it matter that one comes from Rome and the other from Judea?" ("¿Por qué no hablar en términos de dos seres humanos, no importa que uno provenga de Roma y otro de Judea?" [*i*, 64]). This equality is illusory, however, for Bernice is excluded from Rome and is deemed unsuitable for "marriage" to the conqueror. She eventually loses her charm for Titus. Marqués emphasizes here that protection never breeds true love between colony and colonizer. A powerful nation will not support a colony through lean times; it wants the colony only in its prime, when it can be fruitfully exploited. Rome's destruction of the colony's essence is expressed by Bernice: "Oh, Rome conqueror, Rome triumphant, Rome hatefully cruel! You lay waste my land, you kill my people, you destroy my kingdom . . . and now . . . you tear out my heart" ("¡Oh, Roma conquistadora, Roma triunfal, Roma odiosamente cruel! Asolas mi tierra, matas a los míos, destruyes mi reino . . . y ahora . . . me arrancas el corazón" [*iv,* 72]).

The colonizer's reign, however, for Marqués will be short-lived. The subjugated people begin to demystify authority figures. At Titus' coronation, as the masses hail Titus as their Caesar, the Hebrew princess Bernice denounces him as the conqueror of Judea, the destroyer of Jerusalem. The Jews clearly despise the Roman conquerors, and the presence of Jews who have become Christians causes unrest. Titus' lover Flavia predicts a rebellion by converted Jews, reflecting the fears of the senate. This hint of rebellion carries a moral warning for the colonizer: his destructive actions will bring his own ruin as well. The inevitable fall of the imperialist is placed in a larger historical context. Bernice notes at the outset that the once mighty Greece became a colony of Rome and warns Titus at the end that the sun will set on his empire as well: "For lack of that love which we never knew, perhaps the empire which you consider yours will die" ("Por falta de ese amor que no conocimos, quizá morirá el imperio que hoy consideras tuyo" [*x,* 100]). And indeed, the empire was not indestructible.

This drama of mankind unfolds on a relatively bare stage. Marqués fixes the audience's attention on the play's emotional content and keeps physical distractions at a minimum. Even the pomp and circumstance of Titus' coronation is left by Marqués up to the director. The single exception — the festive, cluttered spectacle in Titus' summer palace — is by contrast even more stunning. Marqués juxtaposes actions on a single stage by using platforms. On one platform is Bernice in Judea; on another is Titus in Rome. The actors are briefly "frozen" under spotlights and suddenly begin to move. Bernice seduces the young Marcos (a follower of Christ or Paul of Tarsus), but cries out for Titus. Titus' laughter marks the shift in focus to his platform: he is making love to Flavia, but calls out to Bernice. As the scene ends, the two voices are repeating their cries.

As in *Carnival Outside, Carnival Inside,* Marqués makes use of the mask. Among the Jewish dancers in scene *vii* is a figure in a golden mask, which is dropped in the panic caused by the eruption of Mount Vesuvius. Titus ironically retrieves the mask, for he is unmasking his own life and faces the truth of his dissipation. Later in the play, Bernice refuses to let servants disguise her withered face and gray hair; she rejects a deceptive mask and faces Titus as she really is.

Scene *vii* is particularly innovative. A gauze curtain separates the festive environment of Titus' summer palace from Titus' serious conference with the senators in the foreground. During the conference, the background remains dark. As the conference ends, Titus moves to the background, which once again becomes animated with light, music, voices. Titus' appearance before the senate in scene *viii* is also innovative: the audience becomes the senate, and actors sitting in the audience provide murmurs and cries of protest when Titus threatens to renounce his throne.

In all three biblical dramas, Marqués seems to emphasize the power of love, but his ultimate pessimism suggests that he puts little faith in the solution he proposes. He believes that men inevitably opt for self-interest, manipulating others for their own purposes. In this sense, Marqués views human existence as one of tragic *desamor* or hate. This leads Marqués' audience and reader to wonder if the pattern of human behavior portrayed expresses the author's own pessimism. Does Marqués intend his cynical portrait of humanity to inspire despair? Woud modern man, guilty of the same defects as biblical man, consider the circumstances portrayed as rationales for weak human behavior? Yet, in his essay "Literary Pessimism," Marqués states that a seemingly pessimistic writer can be, and generally is, an optimist.[6] It is precisely his faith in the possibility of change that motivates his pessimistic literary expression. Marqués portrays man's imperfection because he believes that comprehension of human foibles is the initial step to overcoming them. He also dramatizes how man's failure to maintain ideals and the ideology of love ultimately gains him nothing. Isaac's, Saul's, Jonathan's, and David's egotistical behavior only leads to sorrow, ruin, and death. The same is predicted for Titus. Marqués believes that this picture alone should provide catharsis for mankind. The author considers himself a David who, tired of life and men, would never have undertaken the writing of Ecclesiastes had he not wanted to use his bitter wisdom to show men a harsher, but more secure, path to perfection.

The three dramas together demonstrate the complexity that Marqués achieves in his mature work and reflect his continual artistic development. He is able to portray in the context of ancient society the frailties that still stifle the moral development of mankind. The setting and the artistic devices have changed somewhat, but Marqués' political and moral convictions, and his relationship with his audience, have not.

CHAPTER 10

Latest Works and a Conclusion

I   La mirada (The Glance)

IN 1976, Marqués published his second novel, *The Glance,* which
deals with a young man's[1] search for meaning and love in an
essentially absurd world. A student at the University of Puerto
Rico, the youth is faced with a noisy, dirty, urban environment, in
which student bombings, strikes, fires, attacks, and murders are
the order of the day. In spite of good grades, the young man leaves
the university, explaining to his father that the university is a worse
battleground than that of an actual war. He next visits his brother
Humberto, who lives in Washington. Here the young man is faced
with another absurdity: Humberto, an important figure in Washington politics, passes himself off as an Argentinian and refers to
his own brother as a "distant relative." Humberto speaks more
English than Spanish (which Marqués juxtaposes expertly in a dialogue between the two brothers) and has definitely alienated himself from his roots.

Disgusted with his brother's way of life, the young man returns
to Puerto Rico and decides to work on the land. Yet his land's
beauty is sullied by an invasion of hippies. Plans to drive off the invaders are frustrated when the man is invited to join the group.
Under the influence of drugs, the young man injures some of the
hippies and kills a woman. His prison experiences are no less senseless. Attempts to imbue his comrades with culture — the creation
of a dramatic club, a bilingual journal — fail. Prison authorities
cannot allow the inmates to read Marqués' novel *The Eve of Manhood,* because it is considered subversive. The young man is also
victim of a homosexual orgy, an event sanctioned and enjoyed by
guards, who masturbate as they watch the spectacle.

Within this absurd world, the youth does find meaning in a true love. Marqués traces the young man's sexual awakenings: his adolescent masturbation with a friend, Julito; his embarrassment when María, daughter of his dead brother Carlos, catches him naked; his repressed desire to make love to her; the lovemaking with the frivolous wife of a Washington lawyer that is aborted simply because he cannot get his niece out of his mind; and finally, his torrid lovemaking with María in a San Juan hotel. Yet the moment of happiness is brief, for soon afterwards María dies in a senseless nightclub fire — a holocaust that also takes the life of Julito. Marqués seems to inject here the same pessimistic note found in his biblical drama: the world is senseless, filled with violence. Love is either absent, frivolous, or simply cannot survive. Love is personified in the novel in a mysterious, solitary figure who appears in different places: on the beach, on a rock near the sea, in the university. He is described as a Christlike figure who periodically gives the youth a penetrating glance (both the young man and María have seen this figure in a boat in the waters). Yet Marqués signals the impotence of this figure when, on one occasion, he is shown to be castrated.

In a panel discussion at the University of Puerto Rico in September 1976, moderator Nilita Vientos Gastón commented that Marqués' novel appears to be gloomy, that he seems to have lost faith in the Puerto Rican, in the destiny of the island. Indeed, Marqués' young protagonist could be labeled docile. Marqués also ends the novel with a critique of his island, comparing it to a comet that moves in its orbit, but that does not seem to go anywhere. Yet the author disagreed with the comment made by Nilita Vientos Gastón, stating again that his pessimistic expression is indicative of his optimistic sentiments: "A concerned writer," Marqués said, "cannot remain silent." If he did not have faith in the country and its people, he would not be worried about it. "The writer," he said, "must sound the alarm."[2]

Marqués is essentially reporting reality (in his view), whatever that may be. His *The Glance* is a glance at an absurd, ludicrous world; but he is not a nihilist. In the denouement, he has the young man and his father conclude that one still has reason to live. Also, the Christ figure continues to glance at the man in the finale: Marqués seems to tell us that love may be rendered impotent, but its penetrating glance continues to haunt mankind.

To criticize reality, Marqués employs a bombastic, expressionistic style, already seen in his drama *Carnival Outside, Carnival*

Inside. Inserted into these rapid fire descriptions, however, is an element of humor. Describing university life, Marqués gives us a picture of typical telephone conversations in public phone booths. Such places are witness to endless hours (for only ten cents) of amorous declarations; arguments because the "pill" was not used or because the husband had not left the night before at the usual hour; complaints about foreclosed mortgages or the car with the dead battery; the word-for-word dictation of the stolen chemistry exam; the "cooing" of homosexuals; the appointment made with the young female "scholar," who still has not received her "degree" in prostitution; the cursing when one cannot get a dial tone; the cries of joy when one gets back an extra ten cents, and so forth.

Marqués has stated that the structure of this book is zig-zag. The novel indeed has us jump in time and space, jumps that become most pronounced in dream sequences or hallucinations. One complicated hallucination begins after the youth reads a newspaper article describing the kidnapping of the grandson of a millionaire. Under the influence of drugs, the young man imagines himself and Julito implicated in this crime. The youth is suddenly in Venice in a gondola; in the next moment he is riding in a Fiat, en route to a villa. Held captive in the villa is the kidnapped youth. The scene inside the house becomes bizarre: drunkenness; nudity; strains of an eighteenth century minuet; snatches of conversation in English, Spanish, French, Italian; the castration of the kidnapped youth, whose genitals are then sent to his mother. The hallucination next shifts to the horrified mother who, after viewing the organs, retreats backward and falls from a banister to her death.

The shifts in time and place are also coupled with changes in identity. Under the influence of drugs, the youth becomes the mythological Cronus who decapitates Gea and then castrates Uranus. In his hallucination, the marijuana cigarettes become daggers, the hippies' guitars, torches. The castrated Uranus is next seen as the impotent Christ figure and then as the emasculated kidnapped grandson. The kidnapped youth's dead mother in the hallucination provides the transition to the next scene, in which we are at the wake of the protagonist's own mother.

The zig-zag structure, although at times confusing, is at best a clear reflection of Marqués' vision of an absurd world. The confusing nature of dream scenes reflects man's anxieties with respect to the confused world in which he lives. The castration, which has been labeled pornographic, is actually symbolic: it signals man's impotence within this ridiculous world. Moreover, it points to man's powerlessness because he in turn renders sterile love — the one panacea that, for Marqués, can restore man's "virility."

II Inmersos en el silencio (People Immersed in Silence)

In 1976 Marqués also published a third collection of short stories, *People Immersed in Silence*. This new collection contains twelve of Marqués' short stories written between 1955 and 1975.[3] Included in this volume are stories from his earlier collections: "Passion and Flight of Juan Santos, Wooden Saint Carver"; "The Little Miracle of Saint Anthony"; "Island in Manhattan"; "Death"; and "The Blue Kite." It should be noted that Marqués revised "Juan Santos", omitting from it the last paragraph, criticized by Concha Meléndez. The remaining seven short stories deserve brief commentary.

Three of these narratives see Marqués concerning himself with his island's destiny. The history of Puerto Rico is portrayed symbolically in "Ese mosaico fresco sobre aquel mosaico antiguo" ("That Fresh Mosaic upon that Old Mosaic"). The scene is the present, and a young worker, with orders to demolish an old mansion so that a skyscraper may be built in its place, suddenly sees a woman from a past epoch, dressed in a coffee-colored dress and carrying a parasol, descend from a horsedrawn carriage and enter the mansion. Since the man is often drunk, no one will believe him, and he is ordered to get on with the demolition. Yet he cannot do it, and his boss takes over, while the young man looks on in disbelief and terror. This imminent destruction of the mansion and the woman, in the present, is coupled with shifts to the past. Inside the mansion, Marqués has characters reenact the gradual destruction of his island's liberty, nature, and culture since the turn of the century. Puerto Rico, personified in the figure of the woman, is greeted by a politician and a patriot — the politician suggestive of Luis Muñoz Rivera, who favored protection for his island; and the patriot, José de Diego, who wanted absolute independence for Puerto Rico.[4] Also within the mansion is an architect who constructed the building for the lady, having painted for her on one of its walls a mosaic of coffee leaves and fruit — a man who was in love with the island and who wished to preserve her "nature." Yet the nature surrounding the house disappears, and the mansion falls into disuse. An attempt to convert it into a museum that would house objects of Puerto Rican culture is thwarted by the "son" of the politician (Luis Muñoz Marín). In the denouement of the narrative, the mansion and the woman are finally demolished. The mosaic is left among the ruins, but upon it is a blood stain and broken bones and flesh. By means of the delicate symbolism of the mosaic, Marqués tells us that the destruction of his island is complete.

In "El cazador y el sueño" ("The Hunter and the Dream") and "La ira del resuscitado" ("The Anger of the Resurrected Man"), Marqués again presents Puerto Rico's destiny, but this time, his island's mutilation is avenged. The first story "The Hunter and the Dream" deals with the peace and harmony that, for Marqués, stems from a closeness to the land. He reenacts the Nativity, making it take place in Puerto Rico, and has a generous Puerto Rican peasant offer lodging to the two pilgrims — Mary and Joseph. Marqués underscores the triumph of the man and his family's spirit, generosity, love for their fellow man, in a world in which man's egotism and obsession with material well-being reigns more often than not. When the Child is born, the gifts offered to him are not "material," but the fruits of the land: corn, bananas, and the like. The plot centers about the conversion of a young hunter named Pedro to Christ's doctrine of peace. Offering his slingshot to the Christ Child as a sign of peace, Marqués tells us that Pedro approaches God for the first time.

"The Anger of the Resurrected Man" is a sad sequel to the above short story. Mankind has broken his ties with the land and has gone to the city in search of gold. His god is now the machine and not the land. The Christ figure — described as a young hippie — appears in order to enact justice. The slingshot, offered to him as a sign of peace, is now to become a weapon of war. Christ makes man suffer disillusionment: The Puerto Rican does not find gold in the city; his land withers; his new gods abandon him. The biblical warning that Marqués quoted in his drama *Death* — the wrath of God descending on a nation built on false bases — becomes a reality in this narrative.

The two stories contain contrasting stylistic devices, to suggest harmony in the first and discord, suffering in the second. In "The Hunter," nature is given life: Mary infuses life into a dying bird whom Pedro has wounded. In "Anger," in contrast, nature is destroyed: Marqués tells us that man sheds the lamb's blood (the lamb or *cordero* is symbolic of Puerto Rico) in order to appease the god of the machine. In "The Hunter," miracles herald the birth of Christ: a luminous comet breaks into a myriad of stars; Joseph's staff blooms with flowers after the birth of the Child. In "Anger," miracles are absent: Christ refuses to give a mute child the power of speech. In "The Hunter," music suggests the harmony of love, especially when Mary gives new life to the bird. It also heralds Pedro's approach to the Christ Child. In "Anger," we only hear the weeping and wailing of a sorrowful nation that fails to understand what it has done to merit God's wrath.

The three stories taken together demonstrate Marqués' expert manipulation of symbolism and imagery to effect his political and human message. Although germane to Puerto Rico, the allegory bears a message for many nations of the modern-day world, where materialism, treason to one's essence, the absence of love, have cast man into an existential crisis.

In "Final de un sueño" ("End of a Dream"), Marqués transports us to the world of dreams, holding to the Pirandellian notion that illusions are sometimes more "real" than man's reality. In the story, a man dreams of a romantic encounter with a beautiful woman in a hotel restaurant. After he awakens, he feels compelled to drive to the actual hotel, where he experiences the same interlude with the same woman. Yet the beautiful dream becomes an ugly reality, a bizarre nightmare. Minutes before midnight, the young woman rushes to an elevator. The man follows her, and as she leans on his shoulder, the man discovers that he is supporting a dead woman, with a knife stuck in her back. A search is then made for a young blond man — supposedly a hotel elevator operator — who was seen talking to her. This young man is later found dead, floating in a hotel pool.

Marqués expertly manipulates the chimeric element that transports us out of the normal range of time and space. We are kept in suspense, uncertain of time, the reality of the dream, the existence of characters. We believe that the young blond man is an elevator operator; yet the hotel owner swears that his one elevator operator is a youth with an "Afro" hairdo. A man who speaks to the woman in the dream cannot be identified by the protagonist because the man's back is to him. We are only certain that he is wearing a smoking jacket. When the dream is repeated in reality, the young blond man is seen wearing the same jacket. Time loses its meaning in the narrative. When the protagonist returns to his apartment, he

discovers that the ice in a drink he had prepared hours ago has not
yet melted. Marqués shocks us in the story, making us realize that
reality is elusive; we cannot count on the security of reality. The
author makes us take a good look at the incomprehensible nature
of man's total reality, whether in the waking or the sleeping state.

In "El disparo" ("The Shooting"), Marqués presents a man's
enactment of vengeance for the invasion of his land by foreigners.
The reference seems to be to Sirhan Bishara Sirhan, the Arab who,
disgusted with Kennedy's policy with respect to Israel, assassinated
him — a killing viewed by the protagonist as an act of justice. The
story begins right after the fatal shot, and the young man, with the
revolver still in his hand, is apprehended. Hear him is the blood-
stained body of the man he killed and a woman kneeling at his side,
crying that the slain man was innocent. The word "innocent"
evokes a flashback of events that prove Kennedy's "guilt," in
Sirhan's mind. Recalling his idyllic existence on the land, with its
brilliant sun and nature in bloom, Sirhan suddenly remembers the
invasion of his country by uniformed men, who shed blood and
killed Sirhan's brothers. Kennedy defended these uniformed men
who still occupy Sirhan's nation. The man must therefore die. It is
interesting that when Sirhan fires the gun, Marqués has him see not
Kennedy, but the men in uniform once again. In a style employing
the first person narrative and stream of consciousness, Marqués
has Sirhan give us the rationale for his act. Yet Marqués has him
realize that no one will understand the motivation for his deed.
Psychiatrists, in fact, explore his childhood in order to explain the
assassination; others in the story are amazed that a man who is so
"honorable" could do such a "terrible" thing. Marqués here
praises the nationalist act, but sadly comments on the fact that such
heroism is usually incomprehensible to the nationalist's fellow
men.

In "El bastón" ("The Cane"), Marqués has his protagonist
enact justice for another type of oppression: the female domination
of the male members of a family (the suggestion is Marqués' own
family) over several generations. The *bastón*, or cane, a family
heirloom that remains immovable until the denouement, is a silent
witness to four generations of male domination by the female. The
male's main response has been resignation; for example, the protagonist let his mother choose his wife (not the *mestiza* whom he
truly loved, but the rich, white Isabela) and career (he wanted to be
a writer, but instead was forced to become an agriculturalist). Vio-

lence, though, does become prevalent. At first not aimed at the female (the grandfather of the protagonist, tired of his wife's complaints, on one occasion, throws a table with the entire contents of a meal on it through a window), it is soon directed specifically against the woman (the protagonist years later in a similar situation overturns the table on his wife). At present, the protagonist, divorced from his wife, lives in the country with his mother. They each live on separate floors, but the man tells us that the two are joined by an interminable umbilical cord. His mother's constant complaints interrupt his writing. His loneliness, on one occasion, forces him to attempt to talk to his mother about his writing. When he discovers that she is more interested in watching television, and that she has thrown out his rum (drinking seems to be his only comfort), the cane assumes a violent role. The man smashes the television set and presumably hits his mother. The male's vengeance is complete.

The story is presented in flashback, but in zig-zag fashion. There are jumps in time even within the flashback. For example, while remembering his mother's dictation of his wife and career, he recalls a "past" event: the grandfather's hurling of the table through the window; he next relives a "future" event: his own repetition of the episode years later. We return frequently to the present and cast an eye on the immovable cane that will soon assume heroic proportions.

The protagonist's solitude — his children never visit him, he cannot communicate with his mother — reflects Marqués' deep frustration, loneliness, and pessimism. Yet the next short story, also autobiographical, pinpoints Marqués deep, abiding love for mankind.

In "¿Amigo no eres tú yo mismo?" ("Friend, Aren't You me?"), Marqués describes a friend (who is Marqués himself) and explains how this friend transferred from a vocational interest in the land to writing, describing the transfer lyrically as one of no longer opening furrows in the earth but in men's souls. Marqués describes the joys and sorrows of the writer: he lyrically likens joys to the voice of the nightingale; he dramatically describes sorrows as thunderbolts of torment. The author finds in his friend one defect: there is no hate in his heart. Ironically, it is a defect because hate has reigned and prevails today among God's children. And Marqués ironically asks his friend if he is not one of God's children. The author again is juxtaposing the real — hate — and the ideal — love, the latter of which Marqués experiences and which he proposes as the true experience for all of God's children. Marqués' position here makes us wonder if he is not the Christ figure in *The Glance* who is castrated by a society of hate. He seems to be telling us that he and society will gain back their virility only if love prevails. As Marqués stated in the interview about his novel, he is sounding the alarm for all of mankind; and he adds to this his simple solution, which the human race, in Marqués' view, has ignored for centuries.

III   *Conclusion*

Central to the literary production of René Marqués is his ardent determination to make an impact on the social and political outlook of his countrymen. In poetry, fiction, and plays, he dramatizes the subjugation of Puerto Rico both by Spain and by the United States and deplores the internalization of an intolerable power structure by its victims. Marqués attributes this submission to those human instincts that prevail in his works: greed for power and desire for material well-being at any cost. He also attributes submission to the fear that those in power will seek revenge upon those who dare to disrupt the status quo. Marqués shows how the authorities foster dependency upon the United States, squashing utopian or liberation movements as they emerge.[5] Intellectuals, artists, and nationalists either conform with the system or suffer harassment.

Economic dependency inevitably leads to the cultural domination of Puerto Rico by the United States, and Marqués expresses outrage at his countrymen's willingness to barter national identity for economic gain. Marqués laments what he views as their choice of a Calibán existence at the cost of the spirit of Ariel. The theme of the sellout dominates all of his work — whether the setting be contemporary or biblical, whether the genre be poetry or drama, whether the technique be stylized or realistic.

Marqués envisions a more healthy political and cultural existence for Puerto Rico. He urges cultivation of Puerto Rican identification in culture, history, economy, and language, but fervently insists that this will only be possible when U.S. domination is eliminated. Once political sovereignty is achieved, he argues, his countrymen will be able to adapt or reject models from outside Puerto Rico, on the basis of what is best for the total society and not simply on materialistic grounds.

Marqués is not without critics: Juan Angel Silén has questioned Marqués' characterization of the docile Puerto Rican: "René Marqués represents the continuation of an ideology: that of the pseudoscientific writers, which had its greatest expression with Antonio S. Pedreira, in the thirties. It is the ideology of *impotence* in the face of action and that of *lament* in the face of a colonial reality" ("René Marqués representa la continuación de una ideología: la de los escritores seudocientíficos, que tuvo su mayor expresión con Antonio S. Pedreira, en la década de los 30. Es la ideología de la *impotencia* ante la acción y la del *lamento* ante la realidad conlonial").⁶ Silén claims that Marqués has been blinded by the colonial mentality, that he has lost sight of the economic, political, and ideological struggle that is at the core of society.

Marqués might label this view as docile; or he might label it as a thoughtful reaction. This kind of controversy is precisely what Marqués hopes to evoke from his readers and audiences: his literary creations apparently elicited in Silén sufficient indignation to motivate rethinking of crucial social issues in *Toward a Positive View of the Puerto Rican*. Marqués intends to be provocative, and in this sense the effectiveness of his works may be measured by the resistance they meet — by the extent to which they disturb the protectors of the status quo. We have noted the censorship that was exercised against his plays *Juan Bobo and the Lady of the Occident* and *Death Shall Not Enter the Palace*. His countrymen do not unanimously welcome the prescription that Marqués has written for an ailing Puerto Rico, for the prescription demands the sacrificing of security for the sake of intangible values — liberty and cultural integrity.

Puerto Rico's sellout to materialism is accompanied in Marqués' work with the modern world's replacement of spiritual values with mechanization, specialization, and painful alienation. To dramatize this devaluation of human life, Marqués presents man in the charade, mask, and farce that distance him from reality.

Although Marqués endows his characters with seemingly uncontrollable passions, he does not release them from moral and intellectual responsibilities. He asserts that men must guard against engulfment by a single ideology, against the kind of closed existence that obviates new ideas and new outlooks. Marqués' plots often involve situations in which any attempt to view the world from a new perspective is thwarted by a corrupt value system. The hermetically sealed existences created by Marqués may be individual or social in nature, but in either case, they must be recognized and thoroughly analyzed because they may cause personal and national ruin.

In a larger sense, Marqués offers an alternative way for modern man to deal with reality. He urges the individual to stop worshipping a single system or single ideology as if it were divinely inspired, indeed, as if it were itself a deity. Marqués points to another more intelligent way of living: through constant doubt, to struggle to perfect one's world by looking at it squarely, by examining it thoroughly, by continually considering new ways of looking at it. Failure to do so will result in a "No Exit" situation that will suffocate the individual and therefore society as well.

René Marqués conforms with Dilthey's conception of the writer: "The writer shows the boundless possibilities of looking at life, of evaluating it, and of creatively shaping it anew."[7] Viewing life in terms of man's constant tragic and absurd captivity within confining ideologies, Marqués denounces evil in the hope that man will find a solution: "The somber and anguished questions which the pessimistic writer formulates do not have the evil purpose of sinking man into desperation, into nothingness. He formulates them, on the contrary, as a challenge to the creative capacity of man; they are darts shot to the sleeping conscience of others" ("Las preguntas sombrías y angustiosas que formula el escritor pesimista no llevan el propósito malvado de hundir al Hombre en la desesperación, en la nada. Las formula, por el contrario, como un reto a la capacidad creadora del Hombre; son dardos disparados a la conciencia dormida de los otros").[8]

Marqués' development as a writer is difficult to judge in the genre of poetry, where he produced only one book. Marqués' novel *The Eve of Manhood,* written just prior to a peak period of drama, reflects the artistic expertise of that moment. Some of these stylistic devices carried over into his much later novel, *The Glance,* are — symbolism, flashback, the presentation of reality through the psyche of a young man, for example. Yet the later novel seems less well realized, because the zig-zag presentation of reality and change in identities, time, and space, although reflecting the flow of consciousness of the protagonist, are at times confusing to the reader.

Marqués' maturation as a writer becomes more evident in a chronological view of his short stories and drama. His short stories develop from the traditional narrative to the narrative that unfolds in the psyche of the protagonist and indicates a stream of consciousness. Within his varied dramatic style — naturalistic-realistic theater, allegory, pantomime, tragedy, poetic theater, Theater of the Absurd, historical drama, farce — Marqués' drama evinces an evolution from melodrama and the presentation of black and white solutions of conflicts to dramas of more subtle denouement. As Marqués increases the subtlety of the problems and solutions, so also his characters become increasingly complex — showing human merits and shortcomings. The development in this direction is fairly constant, with only minor slips into melodrama (*Mariana, or the Dawn*) and biting political outbursts (*Carnival Outside, Carnival Inside*). As his artistry becomes more sophisticated, Marqués runs into a dilemma with thesis, for his message is not as sharply delineated. It forces the audience to muse upon the drama's subtlety and to reach its own conclusions. This may account for Marqués' choosing thesis over art in a drama of his mature period — *Mariana, or the Dawn* — where the dramatist preferred to unequivocally exhort his islanders on the centennial of the Lares insurrection, rather than cloud his purpose with artistry and subtlety.

Marqués' theater involves not only the interaction of his characters in dialogue, but also in gestures and tableau representations highly charged with emotion. The elaborate stage devices in his drama gradually give way to a more spartan stage setting in later plays. Marqués also creates strong visual impressions, using concrete objects to dramatize his social message. At the same time, his theater is highly auditory: music is utilized to create mood, and Marqués' use of sound effects becomes increasingly refined in his work. Marqués' even appealed to the olfactory sense: in *Titus and Bernice* his stage directions call for incense.

Marqués theater also uses a free flow of time. The drama may begin with the denouement, and then depict in flashback the events that lead to this finale. Or it begins in the midst of things, and again the flashback fills in the character's history, the circumstances that make him act as he does in the present and as he will in the future. The use of cinematic technique ranges from the simple flashback in *The Sun and the MacDonalds* to the more complex flashback within a flashback in *A Blue Child for that Shadow.*

These and other stylistic devices (symbolism, nature imagery, contrasts, parallelism) are not confined to one genre and are constantly refined in his work. Marqués often crosses genres: his short stories are essentially dramatic; in fact, he adapted several of his short stories into plays. A strong poetic vein runs throughout his drama and is found as well in his autobiographical novel.

Marqués is continually innovating, reworking themes and stylistic devices in several genres. He is most versatile and daring in the drama, which comprises most of his literary output. In plays, he not only reworks material, but also introduces new elements.

The critic Arcadio Díaz Quiñones has stated that Marqués is a man who lives alert to his times, preoccupied with and attentive always to the problems of his country.[9] We might add that this alertness to the social problems of his Puerto Rico and the modern world is coupled with Marqués' awareness of both traditional and vanguard modes of literary expression that help him portray these social defects. For Marqués, perfection lies not in man's satisfaction with his world, but in his relentness quest for new worlds and in his use of all his resources to create these new horizons.

Notes and References

Preface

1. See bibliography for a complete listing of Marqués' works. In addition to three collections of his short stories, Marqués also edited a fourth collection: *Cuentos puertorriqueños de hoy* (Modern Puerto Rican Short Stories).

2. For a detailed discussion of Puerto Rican dependency, see Gordon K. Lewis, *Puerto Rico, Freedom and Power in the Caribbean,* Harper Torchbooks (New York: Harper and Row, 1968). Also, Manuel Maldonado Denis, *Puerto Rico: mito y realidad (Puerto Rico: Myth and Reality* [San Juan: Ediciones Peninsula, 1969], and his *Puerto Rico, una interpretación histórico-social (Puerto Rico, a Socio-historical Interpretation),* 2nd. ed. (México City: Siglo veintiuno Editores, S.A., 1969).

3. Lewis, p. 352.

4. See prologue by F. Vázquez Alamo to Marqués' *Teatro (Theater* [Río Piedras: Editorial Cultural, Inc., 1971], II, 7–12.

Chapter One

1. The dates given in the text are dates of composition.

2. *Otro día nuestro* (San Juan, 1955), pp. 19–20. The Nationalist Party of the 1930s advocated violence and terrorist activity as a means to achieve independence. This party became defunct in the elections of 1932, when it only won two percent of the votes cast. Nationalist agitation continued, however, and is carried out even today by such groups as FALN, FURIA, and MIRA, who claim responsibility for recent bombings in New York and on the island. The Independence Party, in contrast, founded in 1946, still campaigns peacefully for independence from the United States. Most Puerto Ricans, including most *Independentistas,* denounce nationalist terrorism, but the radicals insist that violence is the only way to make yourself heard. Although not a nationalist, Marqués portrays and evokes sympathy for nationalist activities in his work. At the same time, he criticizes the nationalist suicidal impulse, maintaining that a deathwish seems sometimes to override ideological considerations. Marqués attributes the limited success of the nationalist movement in Puerto Rico not only to oppression, but also to its failure to maintain cohesive revolutionary doctrine.

3. The date of this drama is uncertain. Editors list it as being written in 1960; yet Marqués read it to a small group (including C. Pilditch) in 1962, introducing it as his latest work.

4. *Peregrinación (Pilgrimage)* (Arecibo, 1944), p. 39.

Chapter Two

1. The late 1920s and the decade of the 1930s is suggested. Mention is made of the hurricane of San Felipe, which occurred in September 1928. Also, for references to the depression and prohibition, see Chapter XXV of *La víspera del hombre (The Eve of Manhood)*, 2nd ed. (Río Piedras: Editorial Cultural, Inc., 1970). Subsequent page numbers following quotations from this work will refer to this edition.

2. See Tomás Blanco, *Prontuario histórico de Puerto Rico (Historical Resume of Puerto Rico)*, 6th ed. (San Juan: Instituto de Cultura Puertorriqueña, 1970), pp. 121–22. The author cites the historians Diffie.

3. Don Rafa is actually Pirulo's father. Because he wishes to conceal his true relationship to Pirulo, Don Rafa functions in the role of *padrino* throughout the novel. Father Joseph Fitzpatrick characterizes the padrino in *Puerto Rican Americans, The Meaning of Migration to the Mainland* (Englewood Cliffs, New Jersey: Prentice-Hall, Inc., 1971), p. 91: "The padrino is a person, strategically placed in a higher position of the social structure, who has a personal relationship with the poorer person in which he provides employment, assistance at time of need.... The padrino is really the intermediary between the poor person, who has neither sophistication nor influence, and the larger society of law, government, employment, and service. He is a strategic helper in times of need, but the possibilities of exploitation in this relationship are very great." Don Rafa, in the guise of patron, safeguards Pirulo's well-being and fosters his education.

4. Blanco (p. 91) supplies the basic details. On September 23, 1868, the Venezuelan Manuel Rojas and the North American Matthew Bruckman gathered some four hundred men in the town of Lares and proclaimed the independence of Puerto Rico. After naming a provisional government, they left the town of San Sebastián del Pepino, with the purpose of taking it over. The next day, in Pepino, the revolt was terminated when it was learned that military forces were arriving from Aguadilla. Many arrests were made, and seven of the leaders were condemned to death.

5. The North Americanization of school teachers and the indoctrination of students — in a setting filled with portraits of Washington or Johnson — is caricatured by Marqués in his essay "El ruido y la furia de los críticos del señor Kazin" ("The Noise and Fury of the Critics of Mr. Kazin"). See *Ensayos (Essays)* (1953–1971), 2nd ed. rev. (Río Piedras: Editorial Antillana, 1972), pp. 119–30. (The caricature is presented on p. 125). When referring to Marqués' essays, we will cite from this edition.

6. Lewis, pp. 64, 382, 383.

7. Enrique A. Laguerre, *Pulso de Puerto Rico (Pulse of Puerto Rico),* in *Obras completas (Complete Works* [San Juan: Instituto de Cultura Puertorriqueña, 1964]), III, 416, 415, 417. For a recent treatment of apathy toward, and ignorance of, local realities, see Pedro Juan Soto, *El francotirador (The Guerilla Fighter* [México City: Editorial Joaquín Moritz, S.A., 1969]).

8. Marqués has acknowledged that the novel is semiautobiographical; Doña Irene, for example, is a portrait of the author's grandmother.

9. Lita at first suggests that Raúl is the father of her unborn child. However, when she is fleeing from her crazed stepmother, Lita hints to Pirulo that Raúl may not have fathered the child: "And if she kills me ... I want you to know ... I want to tell you ... Raúl ... did not ..." ("Y si me mata ... Quiero que sepas ... Quiero decírtelo ... Raúl ... no ..." [p. 275]). She is interrupted by her stepmother's approach and is forced to flee.

Chapter Three

1. *Peregrinación (Pilgrimage),* pp. 5-6. Further references will be given in the text.

2. Lewis, p. 100: "since the island formed part of the Caribbean ocean frontier..., increasingly after 1940 the interest of Washington in the region became overwhelmingly strategic in character. The routines of war and blockade, of organizing vital supplies, civilian defense measures, military recruiting and training, replaced those of socioeconomic reorganization." Yet Marqués admits that Puerto Rico benefited economically during World War II in his "Pesimismo literario y optimismo político: su coexistencia en el Puerto Rico actual" ("Literary Pessimism and Political Optimism in Present-day Puerto Rico [*Ensayos, (Essays),* p. 56]). Without inflation and the commercial and military necessities of the United States in World War II, the economic development of Puerto Rico would have never reached such spectacular achievements during the decade of the 1940s.

3. In the poem "El milagro de mi valle" ("My Valley's Miracle"), Marqués' vitality seems to be restored, and he can offer to his love the life, flourish, and bloom of his own valley. This poem appears in the section "Al amor" ("To Love").

4. "Walking Around" is a poem from Neruda's *Residencia en la tierra,* Volume II (1931-1935).

5. Marqués is certainly conscious of the fact that neither poetry nor drama appeal to large editorial houses (see *Ensayos [Essays,]* p. 243). Marketability cannot therefore be his central consideration in terms of his choice of genre. Marqués' social mission as a writer undoubtedly directed him toward theater as the best medium for confronting people with a mir-

ror of their lives.

Chapter Four

1. Lewis, pp. 115–16. For a more detailed discussion of Operation Bootstrap, see pp. 113–33.

2. Discontent flared into violence by the Nationalist party in 1935 and 1936.

3. Cándido Oliveras left the post at the end of 1964. He was replaced in 1966 by Doctor Angel Quintero Alfaro. The 1970s still witness a concern in Puerto Rico with the teaching of English, especially in the elementary schools. In an interview, recorded in *El Mundo* on April 28, 1974, the secretary of public education, Dr. Ramón A. Cruz, explained the objectives and function of public schools, including the improvement of teaching English. He called for programs to fit the needs of those children whose first language is English, that is, children raised on the mainland whose parents have returned to Puerto Rico. At Washington in March 1974, Cruz called for bilingual education in the mainland cities and requested funds to implement such programs in Puerto Rico's high schools and grade schools. He promised bilingual education with Spanish as the first language, but with enough stress on English so that a graduate is competent in the language (see *San Juan Star,* March 13, 1974). Jaime Benítez participated in this appeal, stating that actual funds for bilingual education are low.

Eduardo Seda Bonilla, in his *Requiem por una cultura (Requiem for a Culture* [Río Piedras: Editorial Edil, Inc., 1970]), p. 115, points out the use of the vernacular in public schools, among poor and lower middle class pupils, as against the tendency toward English usage in private schools that cater to the middle, upper middle, and elite classes and therefore evidence more resistance to the mother tongue. The author refers to the 1965 report of Eladio Rodríguez Otero to the Commission on the Status of Puerto Rico. The situation described remains intact. In his essay "The Docile Puerto Rican," Marqués attacks the Catholic church's support of English for social use (*Essays,* p. 180).

4. Clarence Senior is the author of *The Puerto Ricans* (Chicago: Quadrangle Books, 1965).

5. Marqués stresses in this essay that Puerto Rico is already part of the Occidental world and therefore does not need to be "Occidentalized": "Are we perhaps heirs of an oriental culture? Are we not part of the Occidental world? Is it possible to speak of an anti-Occidental Puerto Rican?" ("¿Somos acaso herederos de una cultural oriental? ¿No formamos parte de Occidente? ¿Es posible un puertorriqueño anti-occidental?" [p. 43]).

For a detailed discussion of the Americanization of the University of Puerto Rico, see Lewis, pp. 393–96; 406. Jaime Benítez was removed from his post in November 1971. Succeeding him as president and rector were Amador Covas and Pedro José Rivera. Arturo Morales-Carrión became president in late 1973. Lifelong member of the Partido Popular Democrático (Popular Democratic party), he challenged Jaime Benítez for the nomination for resident commissioner (1972). His appointment as president was approved by Governor Hernández Colón and Jaime Benítez, but was criticized by Rubén Berríos, president of the Puerto Rican Independence party, who contended that the nomination did not represent the will of the majority of the University of Puerto Rico community. Student activists opposed appointment of Ismael Rodríguez Bou as rector of the Río Piedras campus in April 1974, accusing him of helping to formulate imperialistic policies in Latin American universities (see *San Juan Star,* December 5, 1973, and February 27, 1974; also, *El mundo,* April 27, 1974).

6. Maldonado Denis attempts to destroy the myth of United States "superiority" by making the islanders aware of their natural resources — sugar cane, coffee, tobacco, nickel, cobalt, copper. He urges Puerto Ricans to be aware of, and to resist, U.S. control of such resources. He also tries to destroy the myth that Puerto Rico's prosperity is rooted in increased investment of U.S. capital, stating that the greater part of industrial gains leave Puerto Rico and that the North American investors take from Puerto Rico much more than that which they invest (*Puerto Rico: Myth and Reality,* pp. 63, 65, 67).

7. Marqués also notes (p. 162) that Puerto Rico is the Catholic country with the highest incidence of suicides in the world. His source for this statistic is the United Nations Demographic Yearbook for 1951.

8. Marqués is quick to mention (pp. 163–64) that his analysis of the suicidal impulse of the nationalist can neither overshadow nor diminish the importance of the nationalist movement in contemporary Puerto Rican political History. He feels that some reforms under the commonwealth are a product of the fear that nationalism provoked in the 1950s.

9. Marqués also points out in this essay (pp. 78–79) that a study made on positive versus negative literature concluded that readers identify more, intellectually and emotionally, with pessimistic literature.

10. Juan Angel Silén, *Hacia una visión positiva del puertorriqueño (Toward a Positive View of the Puerto Rican)* (Río Piedras: Editorial Edil, Inc., 1970).

Chapter Five

1. Along with *Another Day of Ours* and *In a City Called San Juan,* 3rd ed. (Río Piedras: Editorial Cultural, Inc., 1970), Marqués also edited *Cuentos puertorriqueños de hoy (Modern Puerto Rican Short Stories),* 2nd ed. (Río Piedras: Editorial Cultural, 1959), which includes two of his own short stories: "Another Day of Ours" and "In the Stern, There Lies a Body." Page numbers following quotations from these works refer to

these editions. The short stories "Another Day of Ours," "The Oath," and "Fear" of *Another Day of Ours* also appear in Marqués' second collection, *In a City Called San Juan.* In 1976 Marqués published a third collection of short stories, *Inmersos en el silencio* (*People Immersed in Silence* [Río Piedras: Editorial Antillana, 1976]), discussed in Chapter 10.

2. Marqués may be referring to the violent university strike of 1948, which resulted in the expulsion of student leaders, as well as several of the younger and more brilliant professors (see "Literary Pessimism...," *Essays,* p. 56).

3. This paragraph has also been criticized by Concha Meléndez. See Concha Meléndez, "Cuentos de René Marqués," "René Marqués' Short Stories" Prologue to *Another Day of Ours,* pp. 7–18.

4. See "The Docile Puerto Rican," *Essays,* p. 161.

5. See *Modern Puerto Rican Short Stories,* p. 107.

6. Marqués portrays the Ponce massacre: on Palm Sunday 1937, armed police in Ponce opened fire on unarmed nationalist demonstrators.

7. Maldonado Denis (*Puerto Rico: Myth and Reality,* p. 61) states that the North Americans have thirteen military bases on the island — two of them thermonuclear. He also asserts that the Pentagon is the largest landed estate owner in Puerto Rico, occupying more than one hundred thousand acres of arable land.

Chapter Six

1. *Teatro,* II, 44. Subsequent page numbers following quotations from this work will refer to this edition. Contains *Man and his Dreams* and *The Sun and the MacDonalds.*

2. Marqués' stance against established religion is expressed in *Modern Puerto Rican Short Stories,* pp. 105–106: "I believe in what is religious more than in religion. I possess a rich Catholic background that I have no intention of renouncing. Nevertheless, my temperament — perhaps more than my reason — prohibits me from following the dogmatic severity of Roman Catholicism almost as much as it prohibits me from accepting the puritannical hypocrisy of Anglo-Saxon Protestantism. In spite of which, I believe I am essentially a religious spirit." ("Creo en lo religioso más que en la religión. Poseo un rico trasfondo católico del que no tengo intención alguna de renegar. Sin embargo, mi temperamento — quizás más que mi razón — me impide seguir el rigor dogmático del Catolicismo romano casi tanto como me impide aceptar la hipocresía puritana del Protestantismo anglosajón. A pesar de lo cual creo entender que soy, de modo esencial, un espíritu profundamente religioso".)

Chapter Seven

1. "Origen y enfoque de un tema puertorriqueño" ("Origin and Focus

of a Puerto Rican Theme"), Program of the Fourth Puerto Rican Theater Festival (San Juan, 1961), p. 6.

2. *The Oxcart,* trans. by Charles Pilditch (New York: Charles Scribner's Sons, 1969), I, 13. Subsequent page numbers following quotations from this work will refer to this edition.

3. Lewis, pp. 114, 115.

4. When Luis hesitates over the move, it is Doña Gabriela who makes the decision: "No! We're going. We're leaving this accursed place for good today. If the rest of you want to stay, you can. I'm going. And you are too, Luis." (I, 40).

5. Luis' affair with Doña Isa does not dishonor his family, since a man's machismo is highly valued in Puerto Rican culture. This is not true of an unmarried woman's loss of virginity or of a married woman's adultery. Doña Gabriela becomes indignant at the dishonor that Doña Isa has brought to her home. For a discussion of the social significance of machismo and virginity, see Eugenio Fernández Méndez, *La identidad y la cultura (Identity and Culture)* 2nd ed. (San Juan: Instituto de Cultura Puertorriqueña, 1970).

6. Aristotle characterized the tragic hero as a man "whose misfortune is brought about not by vice or depravity, but by some error or frailty." He added that "the defect lay in the inherent one-sidedness of all human action in an imperfect world." See S. H. Butcher, trans., *Aristotle's Theory of Poetry and Fine Art,* 4th ed. (New York: Dover Publications, Inc., 1951), pp. 45, 310.

7. Frank Dauster, "The Theater of René Marqués," *Symposium* (Spring 1964), p. 38, criticizes the episodic quality of Act III.

8. María Teresa Babín, "Apuntes sobre *La carreta*" ("Notes on *The Oxcart*"), *La carreta,* 5th ed. (Río Piedras: Editorial Cultural, Inc., 1963), p. xi, believes that adherence to standard, literary Spanish, far from undermining the rendering of Puerto Rican culture, would in fact attract more readers.

9. Juan Bobo, a Puerto Rican folklore character, is typically naive, infantile, attracted to the new and strange. Marqués transforms him into a sensitive being in his drama. Francisco Manrique Cabrera, *Historia de la literatura puertorriqueña (History of Peurto Rican Literature)* (Río Piedras: Editorial Cultural, Inc., 1969), p. 62, notes that even in folklore, Juan Bobo often functioned as an *idiot savant* who played the fool to deceive others. For further discussion of the folkloric Juan, see María Teresa Babín, *La cultura de Puerto Rico (Peurto Rican Culture)* (San Juan: Instituto de Cultura Puertorriqueña, 1970), pp. 81–84.

10. *Juan Bobo y la Dama de Occidente (Juan Bobo and the Lady of the Occident),* 2nd ed. (Río Piedras, Editorial Antillana, 1971), p. 30.

11. Maxine Gordon, "Cultural Aspects of Puerto Rico's Race Problem," *American Sociological Review,* XV (June 1950), p. 390.

12. On the censorship of this play, see "Origen, vida, sueño apacible y

despertar violento de una pantomima: 1955-1971" ("Origin, Life, Pleasant Dream and Violent Awakening from a Pantomime: 1955-1971") in *Juan Bobo,* pp. 11-12.

13. *Essays,* pp. 80-81. Consciousness of the cultural damage done to Puerto Rico by foreign domination was heightened by Luis Muñoz Marín, when he called for Operación Serenidad (Operation Serenity), a reemphasis on the traditional culture, values and qualities of Puerto Rican life. Yet in 1971 Marqués wrote the essay "Origin, Life, Pleasant Dream" to introduce a revision of *Juan Bobo.* He argued that the Puerto Rican educational system remained unchanged: Jaime Benítez still reigned in the university; Puerto Rico was still dominated by "Occidental" culture.

14. The radical leader Luis Muñoz Marín began his political career in the second half of the 1920s as an exponent of the socialist and nationalist creed; he later supported Albizu Campos in 1932. Yet even in 1932, Luis Muñoz Marín's political position had begun to shift. He began to support reforms within the existing order, favoring economic improvement while ignoring the issue of Puerto Rico's political status. In 1938, two years after Muñoz Marín's party (Partido Popular Democrático [Popular Democratic party]) took power, Muñoz Marín announced to the Puerto Rican people that the status of Puerto Rico would not be an issue in the 1940 elections. He argued that independence would follow as soon as Puerto Rico solved its economic problems. This liberty never materialized, however, since industralization involved economic dependency on the United States. For an account of Muñoz Marín's political activities, see Maldonado Denis, *Puerto Rico: Myth and Reality*, pp. 47-71.

15. This triumverate was featured in *Man and his Dreams,* an earlier Marqués play.

16. *Teatro, I, 2nd ed.* (río Piedras: Editorial Cultural, Inc., 1970), I, 239. contains *The Truncated Suns, A Blue Child for that Shadow,* and *Death shall Not Enter the Palace.* Subsequent page numbers following quotations from this work will refer to this edition.

17. Carlos Solórzano, *Teatro latinoamericano del siglo XX (Twentieth century Latin American Theater)* (Buenos Aires: Ediciones Nueva Visión, 1961), p. 84, argues that in the denouement of *Death Shall Not Enter the Palace,* upon discovering that her fiancé Alberto is going to kill the governor, Casandra chooses to kill her lover and herself. But it is more likely that Alberto is the victim of a struggle for the gun. It would be inconsistent with the play's moral and dramatic logic for Casandra to kill Alberto, since the two ultimately shared the same ideals.

18. In his youth, Muñoz Marín actually wrote poetry while living in New York's Greenwich Village. See Earl Parker Hanson, *Puerto Rico: Land of Wonders* (New York: Alfred A. Knopf, 1960), pp. 55, 84-85.

19. See D. L. Shaw, "René Marqués' *La muerte no entrará en palacio:* An Analysis," *Latin American Theater Review,* II, i (Fall 1968), 31-38.

20. Marqués realistically portrays historical events in Puerto Rico

under Luis Muñoz Marín, but then creates the fictional assassination of the governor.

21. *Teatro,* I. René Marqués has worked with the content of this drama in two short stories: "The Child in the Tree" and "The Living Room," which appear in *In A City Called San Juan.*

22. *La casa sin reloj (The House Without a Clock)* (Xalapa: Universidad Veracruzana, 1962), II, 96. Subsequent page numbers following quotations from this work will refer to this edition.

23. Martin Esslin, *Theater of the Absurd,* Anchor Books, rev. ed. (New York: Doubleday and Co., Inc., 1961), pp. 372, 329, discusses the reconciliation between "an ideological, politically oriented theatre and the seemingly apolitical, antiideological Theater of the Absurd." He notes that Brecht, like Adamov, rejected the Theater of the Absurd in his later work. "Like Adamov, he turned towards a socially committed and, at least in outward intention, fully rational theatre. Yet Brecht's case also shows that the irrational Theatre of the Absurd and the highly purposeful politically committed play are not so much irreconcilable contradictions as, rather, the obverse and reverse side of the same medal. In Brecht's case, the neurosis and despair that were given free rein in his anarchic and grotesque period continued as actively and as powerfully behind the rational facade of his political theatre, and provide most of its poetic impact."

24. *Ibid.,* p. 353. "The Theatre of the Absurd merely communicates one poet's intimate and personal intuition of the human situation, his own *sense of being,* his individual vision of the world. This is the *subject matter* of the Theatre of the Absurd, and it determines its form, which must, of necessity, represent a convention of stage basically different from the 'realistic' theatre of our time."

25. *Ibid.,* p. 352. Behind "the satirical exposure of the absurdity of inauthentic ways of life," the Theatre of the Absurd has a more positive purpose: to provide catharsis, to reveal to man that he cannot accept "closed systems of values" and that, hence, "life must be faced in its ultimate stark reality."

26. *Ibid.,* p. 354. "The action in a play of the Theatre of the Absurd is not intended to tell a story but to communicate a pattern of poetic images. To give but one example: things happen in *Waiting for Godot,* but these happenings do not constitute a plot or story; they are an image of Beckett's intuition that *nothing really ever happens* in man's existence."

27. *Ibid.,* pp. 328, 300. Commenting on verbal nonsense in the plays of Ring Lardner, Esslin states: "For all its amiable inconsequence, the dialogue of these short plays, like most writing based on free association, has its psychological relevance in returning again and again to basic human relations. In *The Tridget of Griva,* one of the characters (who are sitting in rowboats pretending to be fish) asks another, "What was your mother's name before she was married?' and receives the reply, 'I didn't know her

then.' "

28. Germaine Brée, *Camus,* rev. ed., Harbinger Books (New York: Harcourt, Brace and World, Inc., 1964), p. 200, states that Camus forces us to admit that life "is both absurd and, for each of us, infinitely valuable. Its very value is enhanced by an acute consciousness of its irreducibility to human understanding." She continues (p. 210): "Our revolt against the absurd begins when our consciousness of its existence is followed by the refusal to be obsessed and paralyzed by it."

29. Micaela creates a new social reality for herself that transcends her husband's passivity. This recalls the surrealist tendency and *creacionismo* of Chilean poet Vicente Huidobro, who juxtaposed elements of reality to give them new relationships to one another and therefore new meaning. See *Altazor,* in *La poesía hispanoamericana desde el modernismo (Latin American Poetry Since Modernism),* ed. by Eugenio Florit and José Olivio Jiménez (New York: Appleton-Century Crofts, 1968), pp. 266–67; Huidobro associates the *golondrina* (swallow) with *día* (day) and *clima* (climate), coining such neologisms as *"golondía"* and *golonclima."*

30. Esslin, p. 365.

31. For an account of the events leading to the insurrection, see Antonio Rivera, *Acercándonos al Grito de Lares (Approaching the Cry of Lares* [San Juan: Instituto de Cultura Puertorriqueña, 1958]). Antonio Rivera attributes the fall of the revolutionary movement to disunity, inadequate leadership, and ultimately to betrayal — conditions which Marqués portrays in his drama. *Mariana o el alba (Mariana or the Dawn)* (Río Piedras: Editorial Antillana, 1968). Subsequent page numbers following quotations from this work will refer to this edition.

32. See Luis Lloréns Torres, *El Grito de Lares (The Cry of Lares),* 2nd ed. (San Juan: Editorial Cordillera, Inc., 1967).

33. Prior to the revolution, an attempt at military sedition occurred in San Juan. Many of the intellectuals, including Ramón Emeterio Betances, were judged guilty by association and exiled. Betances was accused of trying to destroy Spain's domination in America and was considered an advocate of United States' protection.

34. Reinaldo Domenech, a native Puerto Rican, comes to warn Mariana of rumors concerning her political activity before the insurrection and affirms the importance of loyalty to the Spanish Crown. There are fears that he may be a spy.

35. The laws of the epoch actually would not have permitted a marriage between Rosaura and Redención, even though the slave had been liberated by his masters. A more likely type of interracial marriage, which did exist in colonial days, is explained by Maxine W. Gordon (p. 386):

In Puerto Rican colonial times, family structure (its racial components) and sexual mores were regulated by two major factors: (1) the absence of Spanish female (white) mates for the Spanish colonial soldiers, and (2) the need later to increase the number of slave-workers as the Indian population declined. This decline, rather than feelings of tolerance, brought about the importation of Negro slaves, and promoted union among not two, but three different racial stocks. This more accurately accounts for interracial marriages,.... It further recognizes the basic facts that (1) different cultural conditions determine different family patterning, and (2) that family ties, regardless of race, are more elemental and enduring than those of any other human grouping. Since mixed marriages can be shown to be a function of biological and cultural (i.e., institutional, economic, geopolitical, traditional) factors, we see they do not result from "liberal attitudes."

That Mariana's ideal was not shared by all is evidenced by her words blessing the future union between Redención and Rosaura: "We live in a society with prejudice; beneath an unjust system, not only in the political sphere, but also in the economic and social. Christ's doctrine which was brought to America from Europe, has never been fully practiced in the lands of this hemisphere.... You need extraordinary valor to confront the consequences of your love." ("Vivimos en una sociedad con prejuicios; bajo un sistema que es injusto, no sólo en lo político, sino también en lo económico y lo social. La doctrina de Cristo que la vieja Europa nos trajo a América, jamás se ha practicado plenamente en las tierras de este hemisferio.... Necesitan ustedes valor extraordinario para afrontar las consecuencias de su amor" [II, 134]).

36. As in *The Oxcart,* Marqués attempts to recreate the specific speech pattern of each character, according to his circumstances. The Castillian officer uses *vos* in place of *usted.* And the peasants at times aspirate the final "s" or manifest a Lares' accent.

Chapter Eight

1. *Teatro* I, I, 15. Page numbers following quotations from this work refer to this edition. Marqués has also couched the themes of this drama in the short story "Purification on Christ Street" in his *In a City Called San Juan.*

2. *Carnival Outside, Carnival Inside* (Río Piedras: Editorial Antillana, 1971), I, 28. Subsequent page numbers following quotations from this text will refer to this edition.

3. *Essays,* p. 204.

4. Angelina Morfi, *"El apartamiento:* Nueva ruta en el teatro de René Marqués" (*"The Apartment:* New Route in the Theater of René Marqués"), *Temas del teatro (Themes of the Theater* [Santo Domingo: Editora del Caribe C. por A., 1969]), pp. 112, 108, states that in this drama Marqués presents a disintegrated contemporary man who exists in a vacuum.

5. Marqués notes on the title page of the drama that *apartamiento* has a double meaning: a dwelling, or life lived apart from others. See *El apartamiento* (Barcelona: Ediciones Rumbos, 1966), title page. Subse-

quent page numbers following quotations from this work will refer to this edition.

6. See George Orwell, *1984,* Signet Books (New York: The New American Library, Inc., 1949), p. 17. Orwell created ''Big Brother,'' the epitome of political control and censure, who manipulated his subjects by means of the television screen.

7. This scene is reminiscent of Jean-Paul Sartre's *No Exit,* in which three people are confined to an inferno consisting of a room with no mirrors or windows. The door offers no escape since the infernal heat outside is even more intense than that in the room. They exist without time; it is always day, since one may not turn off the light. See Jean-Paul Sartre, *No exit and Three Other Plays,* Vintage Books (New York: Alfred A. Knopf, Inc., 1949).

The limitations of the individual life are also metaphorically communicated in Harold Pinter's *The Dumb Waiter,* in which two people are confined to a room whose door opens on the unknown. See Harold Pinter, *The Birthday Party and Other Plays* (London: Methuen, 1960). In Ionesco's *Amédée, ou Comment S'En Débarasser (Amédée, or How to Get Rid of It),* Amédée and his wife Madeleine live cut off from the world and have not left their apartment in fifteen years. See Ionesco, *Théatre,* I (Paris: Gallimard, 1954), or the English translation in *Collected Theater,* vol. II (New York: Grove Press, n.d.).

8. Orestes, son of Agamemnon and Clytemnestra, killed his mother and her lover with the aid of his sister Electra, in order to avenge the death of his father. His sacrifice contrasts here with the caution of Elpidio and Carola, who are concerned only with their self-preservation. Orestes appears in the Aeschylus trilogy *Oresteia.*

Chapter Nine

1. *David y Jonatán (David and Jonathan) — Tito y Berenice (Titus and Bernice)* (Rio Piedras: Editorial Antillana, 1970), p. 17. Subsequent page numbers following quotations from this work will refer to this edition.

2. See ''Notas preliminares sobre la leyenda hebrea de Abrahán, Sara e Isaac'' (''Preliminary Notes on the Hebrew Legend of Abraham, Sarah and Isaac'') which forms the prologue to *Sacrificio en el Monte Moriah (Sacrifice on Mount Moriah* (Río Piedras: Editorial Antillana, 1969), for an account and defense of Marqués' poetic license in this drama. Also his ''La leyenda hebrea de Abrahán, Sara e Isaac'' (The Hebraic Legend of Abraham, Sarah and Isaac), *Essays,* pp. 273–306.

3. See epilogue to drama, p. 144.

4. Genesis 26: 6–14.

5. The Hebrew nation has been delivered from Egypt, but is now threatened by the Philistines.

6. *Essays,* p. 80.

Chapter Ten

1. The young man remains nameless throughout the novel. See *La mirada (The Glance)* (Río Piedras: Editorial Antillana, 1976).

2. See Eneid Routte, "The New Puerto Rican Novel: What It Is and What It Isn't," *The San Juan Star,* September 8, 1976.

3. *Inmersos en el silencio (People Imersed in Silence)* (Río Piedras: Editorial Antillana, 1976).

4. In 1916 the Unionist political party split into two factions: one side, led by José de Diego, supported absolute independence for Puerto Rico; the other, headed by Muñoz Rivera, upheld an "independence" under a protectorate.

5. Arguments have also been advanced against statehood: for example, see Lewis (p. 366): "The leading argument ... is that of economic cost. It is part of the *Popular* catechism to assert unequivocally that the automatic removal of the present tax exemption and the immediate application of the federal minimum wage standard (which statehood would involve) would bring about the virtual collapse of the industrialization promotion program." Puerto Rican supporters of the commonwealth reacted to President Ford's surprise proposal on January 1, 1977 that the island commonwealth become the fifty-first state with indignation and distress. Although President Romero Barceló's New Progressive party is committed to statehood, he promised in his campaign not to push for that status during his first term. See *New York Times,* Sunday, January 2, 1977.

6. Silén, p. 70.

7. William Kluback and Martin Weinbaum, trans., *Dilthey's Philosophy of Existence* (London: Vision Press Limited, 1957), p. 38.

8. *Essays*, p. 82. "Literary Pessimism"

9. Arcadio Díaz Quiñones, "El arte del cuento en René Marqués" ("The Art of René Marqués' Short Story"), in *El cuento puertorriqueño en el siglo XX (The Puerto Rican Short Story in the Twentieth Century),* ed. by Facultad de Humanidades (San Juan: Universidad de Puerto Rico, 1963), p. 79.

Selected Bibliography

The following bibliography of Marqués' writings lists booklength publications. His presentations at theater festivals, as well as those short stories and essays that have not been reprinted in his books, have been omitted.

1. Drama

El apartamiento. Barcelona: Ediciones Rumbos, 1966.
La carreta. 5th ed. Río Piedras: Editorial Cultural, Inc., 1963.
La casa sin reloj. Xalapa: Universidad Veracruzana, 1962.
Carnaval afuera, carnaval adentro. Río Piedras: Editorial Antillana, 1971.
David y Jonatán — Tito y Berenice. Río Piedras: Editorial Antillana, 1970.
Juan Bobo y la Dama de Occidente. 2nd ed. Río Piedras: Editorial Antillana, 1971.
Mariana o el alba. Río Piedras: Editorial Antillana, 1968.
Sacrificio en el Monte Moriah. Río Piedras: Editorial Antillana, 1969.
Teatro. Vol. I. 2nd ed. Río Piedras: Editorial Cultural, Inc., 1970. Contains *Los soles truncos, Un niño azul para esa sombra,* and *La muerte no entrará en palacio.*
Teatro. Vol. II. Río Piedras: Editorial Cultural, Inc., 1971. Contains *El hombre y sus sueños* and *El sol y los Mac Donald.*
Teatro. Vol. III. Río Piedras: Editorial Cultural, Inc., 1971. Contains *El apartamiento* and *La casa sin reloj.*
Vía crucis del hombre puertorriqueño (Oratorio). Río Piedras: Editorial Antillana, 1971.

2. Short Stories

Cuentos puertorriqueños de hoy. [ed. Marqués] 2nd ed. Río Piedras: Editorial Cultural, 1959. Contents: selected short stories of Abelardo Díaz Alfaro, José Luis González, René Marqués, Pedro Juan Soto, Edwin Figueroa, José Luis Vivas, Emilio Díaz Valcárcel, Salvador M. de Jesús.

En una ciudad llamada San Juan. 3rd ed. Río Piedras: Editorial Cultural, Inc., 1970.

Inmersos en el silencio. Río Piedras: Editorial Antillana, 1976.

"Ese mosaico fresco sobre aquel mosaico antiguo." Río Piedras: Editorial Cultural, 1975. Special edition of Marqués' short story, complete with artwork, photos illustrating the story, and Puerto Rican history. Also contains two essays about the narrative.

Otro día nuestro. San Juan, 1955.

3. Novel

La mirada. Río Piedras: Editorial Antillana, 1976.

La víspera del hombre. 2nd ed. Río Piedras: Editorial Cultural, Inc., 1970.

4. Essays

Ensayos (1953–1971). 2nd ed. Río Piedras: Editorial Antillana, 1972.

"Origen y enfoque de un Tema puertorriqueño" ("Origin and focus of a Puerto Rican Theme"), Program of the fourth Puerto Rican Theater Festival (San Juan, 1961).

"Origen, vida, sueño apacible y despertar violento de una pantomima: 1955–1971." In *Juan Bobo y la Dama de Occidente.* 2nd ed. Río Piedras: Editorial Antillana, 1971, pp. 9–13.

"Notas preliminares sobre la leyenda hebrea de Abrahán, Sara e Isaac." In *Sacrificio en el Monte Moriah.* Río Piedras: Editorial Antillana, 1969, pp. 21–40.

5. Poetry

Peregrinación. Arecibo, 1944.

6. Translations

Pilditch, Charles. *The Oxcart (La carreta).* New York: Charles Scribner's Sons, 1969.

_____. "In a City Called San Juan." *Review* (Center for InterAmerican Relations), Spring 1976.

_____. "Purification on Cristo Street." *San Juan Review* (San Juan), August 1965.

_____. "The Informer," *Caribbean Review,* Vol. VII, No. 2 (April/May/June 1978), pp. 24–27.

G.R. Coulthard. "Death" ("La muerte"). *Short Story International* (New York), February 1965.

Roach, Eloîse. "The Blue Kite" ("La chiringa azul"). *Americas* (Washington, D.C.: Pan American Union), May 1965.

"Death" ("La muerte"). In G.R. Coulthard. *Caribbean Literature* (An Anthology). London: University of London Press, 1966.

"Island in Manhattan" ("Isla en Manhattan). Trans by Faye Edwards and Gladys Ortiz in *Contemporary Latin American Short Stories,* ed. by Pat McNees Mancini, Fawcett, 1974.

SECONDARY SOURCES

1. Drama

BABÍN, MARÍA TERESA. "Apuntes sobre *La carreta.*" In *La carreta.* 5th ed. Río Piedras: Editorial Cultural, 1963. pp. v–xxi. Study of *La carreta's* thematic composition, dramatic structure, stage devices, characters, and language; also treats this drama's place in the history of Puerto Rican theater and its relationship to the theater of García Lorca and Synge.

BARREDA-TOMÁS, PEDRO M. "Lo universal, lo nacional y lo personal en el teatro de René Marqués." *El teatro en Iberoamérica* (Memoria del duodécimo congreso del Instituto Internacional de Literatura Iberoamericana). México: IILI (1966). As the title indicates, Marqués' political, existential, and personal attitudes are viewed through his drama.

DAUSTER, FRANK. "New Plays of René Marqués." *Hispania,* September 1960, pp. 451–52. Review of *Los soles truncos, La muerte no entrará en palacio,* and *Un niño azul para esa sombra.*

————. "The Theater of René Marqués." *Symposium* (Spring 1964), pp. 35–45. Detailed discussion of Marqués' themes and dramatic devices, focusing especially on the flaws of his drama prior to 1964.

DEL SAZ, AGUSTÍN. "La tierra y la frustración del emigrante. *La carreta* de René Marqués." *Teatro social hispanoamericano,* pp. 107–11. Barcelona: Editorial Labor, S.A., 1967. Analysis of the emigrant's frustration upon severing his ties with the land.

ESPINOSA TORRES, VICTORIA. "El teatro de René Marqués y la escenificación de su obra: *Los soles truncos.*" Ph.D. dissertation, Universidad Nacional Autónoma de México, 1969. Lengthy discussion of European, North American, and Puerto Rican theater; analyzes Marqués' theater, emphasizing literary influences. Earned in the department of theatrical arts, the thesis recounts the actual staging of *Los soles truncos* by Dr. Espinosa Torres.

FERNÁNDEZ, DR. PIRI. "Temas del teatro puertorriqueño." In *El autor dramático,* pp. 153–82. San Juan: Instituto de Cultura Puertorriqueña, Primer Seminario de Dramaturgia, 1963. Includes an analysis of Marqués' *Un niño azul para esa sombra,* as well as dramas by Manuel Méndez Ballester, Emilio Belaval, Gerard Paul Marín, and F. Arriví.

LYDAY, LEÓN F., and WOODYARD, GEORGE W. *Dramatists in Revolt: The New Latin American Theater.* Texas: University of Texas Press, 1976. Contains essays on playwrights of the post–World War II period from

Cuba, México, Argentina, Chile, Brazil, and Puerto Rico (René Marqués). The authors are considered "dramatists in revolt" in a thematic sense — protesting the indignities that various systems impose on modern man — and also in a dramatic configuration — experimenting with techniques in the constant search for viable theatrical forms.

MARTIN, ELEANOR J. "*Carnaval afuera, carnaval adentro:* síntesis del pensamiento social de René Marqués." *Revista Chicano-Riqueña.* Winter 1974, pp. 39-50. Discusses Marqués' critique of Puerto Rican docile acceptance of North American domination of the island at the expense of spiritual values; shows how dramatic conflict centers about the figure of the rebel artist who, upon attempting to instill spiritual values within the status quo, is censured and persecuted.

———. "*Caligula* and *La muerte no entrará en palacio:* A Study in Characterization." *Latin American Theater Review,* Spring 1976, pp. 21-30. Discusses similarities between the dramas of Marqués and Camus and pinpoints Marqués adaptation of a possible source to suit his own political and humanistic purposes.

MORFI, ANGELINA. "*El apartamiento*: Nueva ruta en el teatro de René Marqués." *Temas del teatro,* pp. 107-13. Santo Domingo: Editora del Caribe C. por A., 1969. A study distinguishing Marqués' earlier drama, reflecting a deterministic social vision, with *El apartamiento,* in which man attempts self-definition. The influence of Sartre, Stendahl, and Beckett is noted.

OJEDA, JORGE ARTURO. "Teatro lúcido y didáctico." *Revista de Bellas Artes,* 24 (November-December 1968), 57-62. Deals briefly with Cuzzani's *Sempronio,* Wolff's *Los invasores,* Arreola's *La hora de todos,* Salazar Bondy's *El fabricante de deudas,* and Marqués' *Un niño azul para esa sombra.*

PILDITCH, CHARLES. "La escena puertorriqueña — *Los soles truncos.*" *Asomante,* XVII, 2 (1961), 51-58. On Marqués' *Los soles truncos.*

SHAW, D.L. "René Marqués' *La muerte no entrará en palacio:* An Analysis." *Latin American Theater Review,* II, i (Fall 1968), 31-38. Analysis of *La muerte* as both a play of protest and a tragedy; criticizes Marqués' failure to reconcile his social message with aesthetic aims.

SIEMENS, WILLIAM L. "Assault on the Schizoid Wasteland: René Marqués' *El apartamiento.*" *Latin American Theater Review,* Spring 1974, pp. 17-25. Discusses man's schizoid existence, his isolation, and his acceptance and repression of factors that are designed to end his alienation.

SOLÓRZANO, CARLOS. *Teatro latinoamericano del siglo XX.* Buenos Aires: Ediciones Nueva Visión, 1961. Analysis of trends and representative authors, including the theater of René Marqués'; The author's interpretation of the denouement of *La muerte no entrará en palacio* is questionable.

162   RENÉ MARQUÉS

VÁZQUEZ ALAMO, F. "Análsis prologal." In *David y Jonatán — Tito y Berenice*, pp. 7–15. Río Piedras: Editorial Antillana, 1970. Discussion of Marqués' biblical-historical dramas: *Sacrificio en el Monte Moriah* and *David y Jonatán — Tito y Berenice*, analyzing the two latter plays in terms of dramatic technique, characterization, and application to present-day political issues.

————. "El teatro de René Marqués." In *Sacrificio en el Monte Moriah*, pp. 9–21. Río Piedras: Editorial Antillana, 1969. Groups Marqués' drama into different styles: naturalistic, poetic, and so forth. Summarizes Marqués' constant underlying theme: man's tragic destiny. Discusses themes and techniques of *Sacrificio* and the drama's relationship to the modern age.

2. Short Stories

DÍAZ, QUIÑONES ARCADIO. "El arte del cuento en René Marqués." In *El cuento puertorriqueño en el siglo XX*, ed. Facultad de Humanidades, pp. 75–105. San Juan: Universidad de Puerto Rico, 1963. This article is more inclusive than the title indicates. Contains an account of Marqués' life; an introduction to his theater, novels, and essays; an analysis of Marqués' short stories in *Otro día nuestro*, together with an overall view of the Puerto Rican short story; also contains a detailed analysis of Marqués' short story "Dos vueltas de llave y un arcángel" from *En una ciudad llamada San Juan*.

MELÉNDEZ, CONCHA. "Cuentos de René Marqués." In *Otro día nuestro*, pp. 7–18. San Juan, 1955. Analysis of social and universal themes in *Otro día nuestro*, Marqués' dramatic art in his short stories, and other artistic devices employed by Marqués such as images, flashbacks, psychological processes, and so forth.

————. *El arte del cuento en Puerto Rico*. Las Américas Publishing Co., New York, 1961. Selected short stories of E. Belaval, Tomás Blanco, Edwin Figueroa, José Luis González, René Marqués, and others, with analyses by Concha Meléndez.

3. Novel

NIEVES-COLÓN, MIRNA. "Símbolos y mitos en *La víspera del hombre*." *Románica* (New York University), Spring 1974, pp. 34–38. Analysis of incidents and characters in the novel as expressions of Puerto Rican history and the collective national conscience.

4. General

PILDITCH, C.R. *René Marqués — A Study of His Fiction*. Plus Ultra Educational Publishers, New York, 1977. Introduction to Marqués' work in chronological order with analyses of Marqués' artistic maturation.

For reference to other secondary sources on Marqués (particularly several unpublished Ph.D. dissertations), see Leon F. Lyday and George W. Woodyard. *A Bibliography of Latin American Theater Criticism 1940–1974*. Austin: Institute of Latin American Studies, The University of Texas at Austin, 1976.

Index